D1134232

Great Value Gourmet

Great Value Gourmet

Meals and menus for £1

Paul Gayler

Photographs by Philip Wilkins

Weidenfeld & Nicolson
London

Copyright © Paul Gayler 1996

First published in Great Britain in 1996 by
George Weidenfeld & Nicolson Ltd
The Orion Publishing Group
Orion House
5 Upper St Martin's Lane
London WC2H 9EA

All rights reserved. No part of this publication
may be reproduced, stored in a retrieval
system, or transmitted in any form or by any
means, electronic, mechanical or otherwise,
without the prior permission of the copyright
holder.

British Library Cataloguing-in-Publication Data
A catalogue for this book is available from the
British Library

ISBN 0-297-83601-3

Designed by the Senate
Printed and bound in Italy

Contents

INTRODUCTION

The idea behind this book stemmed from a telephone call I received at the Lanesborough one Friday morning in September 1995. Simon Hinde, the Consumer Affairs Correspondent of the *Sunday Times* rang me to ask if I was prepared to take up the challenge of devising a three-course menu for a family of four, with a budget of just £1. The idea behind this article, he told me, was to bring to people's attention the growing number of discount stores popping up all over Britain, such as Aldi and Lidl, who are offering food prices that are considerably undercutting the well-known supermarket chains.

At first I thought the idea absurd; what could possibly be prepared for £1? However, since my resolve and professionalism had been challenged, I felt that I could not refuse. I set about finding out more. Simon faxed me a list of some 10–12 discounted items he had purchased himself, such as canned beans, canned plum tomatoes, bread, milk, sausages. Even so, the saving grace was that I was allowed a basic storecupboard of ingredients that one might find in any home.

My menu, after much thought and toying with prices on my calculator, consisted of a spicy Mexican-style soup made from baked beans, followed by fusilli with hot dog sausages, tomatoes and herbs and, to finish, a cinnamon-infused baked apple. The whole menu was simplicity itself, well flavoured and reasonably priced, in fact only 87 pence for three courses. A little chilli for the soup, a few dried herbs for the pasta and cinnamon for the apples had worked wonders. I felt quite pleased with myself, but Simon wanted to put the menu to a further test.

He arranged for a family of four to dine at the Lanesborough to eat my 87p meal. The two adults and their two children arrived early one evening at the hotel, a little sceptical of what could be achieved with 100 pence.

After meeting them I returned to the kitchen determined to impress my guests. I'm glad to say the meal proved to be a great success – in fact they even asked for the soup recipe. The children left their plates clean, and having four children of my own, I know that this can sometimes be an achievement in itself.

The publicity that the article in the following weekend's *Sunday Times* attracted was hard to conceive. It made headlines in both American and Mexican newspapers and I received telephone calls from fellow chefs, readers, and even an Italian TV network.

Three months later I began to create this book on similar lines to my challenge; with the aid of a basic storecupboard, I set out to produce menus that vary from £1 for four to £1 per person. The recipes follow my passion for food from around the world, taking their inspiration from Mexico through Europe to the Far East.

Nowadays, thanks to price wars in all the major food outlets, simple but interesting meals are within the grasp of any home cook on a budget. Making the most of seasonal ingredients, the best quality convenience foods and a little imagination, cheap need never mean boring. Used creatively, herbs, spices and condiments add flavour to cheaper cuts of fresh meat and shellfish. Most of the recipes in this book are fairly easy to prepare and incredibly easy on the pocket.

All the recipes are for 4 people unless stated otherwise. I hope that you enjoy trying them.

Paul

THE **STORECUPBOARD**

Home cooking has changed dramatically over the last decade. A steady stream of television programmes celebrating food and foreign travel, backed up by magazine articles and advertisements, has opened our eyes to the many flavours the world has to offer. We also love to eat out and experience new foods at every opportunity. This new-found interest is reflected in our storecupboards; they are now likely to contain many more unusual ingredients – sauces, spices, herbs, different types of rice and pasta – than they would have done a few years ago.

So, what constitutes a basic storecupboard? In a way, it is impossible to summarize, since so much depends on the style of food that you personally enjoy and generally cook at home. However, one thing is for certain: a well-stocked cupboard will open the door to a greater choice of imaginative and exotic meals that the home cook can prepare easily and without further expense.

The following lists constitute what I personally consider a staple storecupboard (in fact, this is more or less what is in my cupboard at home). All the items are featured in the recipes within this book, some far more frequently than others. There's no need to rush out and spend a fortune on stocking up: you will already have many of the ingredients, and others can be bought when you need them.

Everyday basics

These are found in most households:
salt, black pepper (preferably in a pepper
mill, ready to be freshly ground, giving a far
superior flavour to ready-ground pepper),
vegetable oil (buy a neutral-flavoured oil such
as sunflower oil for frying and general use), olive
oil (choose extra virgin olive oil for use in dressings
and sauces), butter (margarine has its uses, but cannot
compare with the flavour of butter), milk (semi-skimmed is
healthier than full-fat), eggs, plain flour, white and brown
sugar, bread, tea, coffee.

Sauces and condiments

These are my favourite flavour enhancers:
good-quality mayonnaise, light soy sauce, tomato
ketchup, tomato purée, pesto sauce, Worcestershire sauce,
Tabasco sauce, anchovy essence, capers in brine, black
olives, white and red wine vinegar, balsamic vinegar,
curry paste, mustard, horseradish, tahini paste.

Chicken, vegetable and beef stock are invaluable in the
kitchen. Some supermarkets now sell good-quality ready-
prepared stocks, but don't be afraid to use a stock cube – it's
fine for many purposes.

Perishables

The basic vegetable rack and fruit bowl could include:
fresh garlic, onions, spring onions, carrots, celery, leeks,
potatoes, fresh ginger, lemons, oranges.

In the refrigerator you might also keep orange
juice, a well-wrapped piece of Parmesan
cheese, natural yoghurt and vegetarian suet.

Perishable in the sense that it gets eaten as
soon as bought, unless well hidden,
chocolate is also useful as an ingredient.
Buy good-quality plain chocolate.

Herb and spice rack

Dried herbs are no substitute for fresh. If at all possible, I recommend that you start your own herb garden, which might include parsley, chives, mint, thyme and sage. The following dried herbs are acceptable if fresh herbs are not available:

bay leaf, thyme, sage, oregano, rosemary, mixed herbs.

Spices from around the world give dishes hot or subtle flavours and great depth of taste. Most spices tend to lose their flavour quite quickly once they have been ground; it is best to buy whole spices (seeds or pods) and grind them yourself just before using them. Alternatively, buy ground spices in small quantities – this is one occasion when it is a false economy to buy in bulk. I use a lot of spices, and the following are some of my favourites:

dried chilli flakes, cayenne pepper, paprika, coriander seeds, cumin, cinnamon, cardamom, nutmeg, cloves, caraway seeds, allspice, turmeric, ground ginger.

Ready-prepared spice mixtures, such as mild curry powder and garam masala, are also useful.

Fennel seeds, sesame seeds and Chinese five-spice powder appear once or twice in this book, and are worth buying if you are particularly fond of Indian or Chinese cooking.

Not just for cakes

Dried fruit and nuts can also be used in savoury dishes, and to add a touch of luxury to simple puddings:

cornflour, baking powder, vanilla essence, yeast (I prefer to use fresh yeast, although dried yeast is easier to keep as a standby – however, don't keep it too long or it may lose its efficacy), raisins, sultanas, prunes, walnut halves, whole and flaked almonds, desiccated coconut.

Cans

These items can be lifesavers, and can easily be converted into new and exciting dishes:

> plum tomatoes (whole and chopped, in various sizes), baked beans, sweetcorn, black beans, cannellini beans, chickpeas, coconut milk, tuna, herrings, sardines, red salmon, anchovy fillets.

Jars

The sweet-toothed may have these already, but several of them can also be used to create savoury dishes:

> good-quality raspberry and apricot jam, redcurrant jelly, orange marmalade, clear honey, maple syrup, peanut butter, molasses.

Pasta and grains

Dried pasta is always a good storecupboard standby and other grains also make satisfying meals:

> long rounded pasta such as spaghetti or linguine; flat noodles such as trenette or tagliatelle; lasagne; small pasta shapes such as fusilli, penne, rigatoni, macaroni; a selection of different types of rice might include long-grain white rice and brown rice (for salads and general purposes), basmati (a particularly fragrant rice with long thin grains), arborio (a rounded grain rice, used to make risotto); other grains that are good for absorbing sauces include polenta (cornmeal) and couscous.

Drinks cabinet

I have long been of the opinion that a dish without booze – in it, with it, or both – is somehow incomplete! One glass for the pot and one for the chef is one of my favourite rules of the kitchen. Joking aside, wines and spirits are invaluable in cooking, especially the following:

> dry white wine, red wine, port, brandy, rum, sherry (a splash of dry sherry is often used in Chinese stir-fries), madeira, beer.

The freezer

I have never been a great advocate of the freezer – it's a point of professional pride – but I do use it to store food that has a very short season when fresh, such as sweetcorn, peas and broad beans. I also find it convenient for storing some pasta, and puff and filo pastry.

It is well worth keeping a stock of ice cream – vanilla and chocolate – to prepare simple desserts and to serve as an accompaniment to hot or cold puddings.

THOUGHTFUL SHOPPING WITH THE **SEASONS**

In a professional kitchen, chefs have access to good-quality raw materials on a daily basis from a varying list of suppliers. This means we can offer our clientele all their favourite foods throughout the year. To many people this may sound wonderful, but I find it somewhat sad, because I believe in the idea of seasonality in foods.

Nowadays, the larger supermarkets are also crammed full of exotic foodstuffs flown in from around the globe, thanks to advances in transportation and the higher expectations of shoppers.

Tomatoes, asparagus and strawberries, for example, are now available throughout the year. Tomatoes have often been picked far too early, therefore they lack flavour because they are underripe. The ripening process continues on their transportation to our markets, instead of on the vine where they should remain until ripe. Taste the difference between these tomatoes and those picked in the height of the summer season. They not only taste better, but they are also less expensive because they are plentiful. The same can be said of strawberries, asparagus and many other ingredients.

A market or greengrocer is far more likely than a supermarket to reflect the seasons – with lower prices when there is a glut. In a nutshell, if you cook with the seasons in mind, you will eat better and spend less. Shop often and plan your menus accordingly.

SPRING

For me the best spring dishes are simple, reflecting the delicacy of the new season, but are nonetheless full of fresh tastes and bright colours.

The glowing reds and distinctive flavours of rhubarb (outdoor-grown by late spring) and beetroot are shown at their best in simple dishes. So too are the many shades of green, characteristic of springtime, found in asparagus, broad beans, peas and fresh young spinach. May is the traditional month for English asparagus, although the exact weeks will depend on the weather. The same is true of broad beans and peas. A few warm weeks will also see British-grown watercress.

New potatoes now seem to be available all year round, but the exquisite Jersey Royals appear only in spring. Unfortunately, they are never cheap.

Purple-sprouting broccoli is a springtime speciality of British growers; look in local markets and farm shops. Also look out for spring cabbage varieties and (unhearted) spring greens.

If you have a good fishmonger, now is the time to buy crab, wild salmon and sea trout (also called salmon trout).

Spring cookery should exploit all the freshness of this abundant season, with minimum artifice.

SUMMER

During the hottest months of the year, seasonal produce and cooking retains the light touch and fresh feel of spring (think of the variety of salad leaves) but has the added punch of sun-ripened flavours and colours: juicy red tomatoes, cherries, strawberries, black-, red- and whitecurrants, golden and purple plums. Gooseberries appear early in the season, raspberries somewhat later.Imported peaches, nectarines and melons are at their prime.

The vegetables of the season are crisp and succulent – courgettes, broccoli, French and runner beans. Globe artichokes are likely to be imported from France. Corn on the cob appears in late summer.

Salads are full of flavour, colour and texture, with British-grown cucumber, celery, tomatoes and fresh raw beetroot.

Locally caught herrings, mackerel and squid join crab on the summer menu.

With a palette of nature's colours, tastes and textures before us, food shopping and cooking is an inexpensive and easy pleasure.

AUTUMN

The countryside seems to turn to gold as we reap the harvests of our fields, orchards and hedgerows, taking advantage of the last warm days for apple and blackberry picking. In autumn we get a choice of traditional apple varieties – don't miss them, as many appear in the shops for a very short season. Pears and several types of plum, including damsons, are also harvested now, as are walnuts and hazelnuts. Imports include luscious pomegranates and figs.

Mussels, clams, scallops and oysters come back into season and cod and plenty of other white fish are good-quality and easily available.

Late summer and early autumn see the arrival of sun-ripened aubergines and peppers; corn on the cob and courgettes continue to be good. Now is also the time to go hunting for wild mushrooms (never eat anything you are in the slightest doubt about). As autumn progresses, cauliflowers and leeks get better.

As the evenings draw in and the weather turns chilly, our thoughts turn to warming bowls of soup, and what better ingredient than autumn's great golden-orange prize, the pumpkin. Other winter squash come in all shapes and sizes, making autumn food buying and cooking just as adventurous as in the summer.

WINTER

The season's tasty and comforting root vegetables are perfect for rustling up casseroles and soups to keep out the cold. With so many different cooking methods – roasting, frying, stewing, mashing – they need never be boring. The variety is almost endless, and includes Jerusalem artichokes, parsnips, turnips, swedes, celeriac, scorzonera and salsify (a long, thin root, sometimes called vegetable oyster).

The brassica family provides the bright colours of Savoy and red cabbages, little Brussels sprouts and good-value curly kale.

Home-grown apples and pears should still be available at good prices. Traditional imports for the Christmas season include cranberries, chestnuts, brazil nuts, pineapples, lychees and a wide variety of citrus fruits.

At the fishmonger, good cheap mussels are joined by bargain sprats and skate.

Cabbages and root vegetables are also the perfect partners to winter's other speciality, game; it's not always expensive, so be ready to take advantage of bargains.

A FEW REMARKS ABOUT **MENU** PLANNING

When thinking about what foods go well together, I often base menus around certain cuisines or styles of cooking (for example, Italian, French, Greek, Thai, Chinese or South American).

Once you understand the spirit of the dish or the style of cooking, feel free to improvise and make changes. Discovering new taste combinations is, for me, the most exciting and creative aspect of cooking.

Remember to plan your time sensibly. For most people, the first attempt at a dish may take twice as long as expected. Plan menus to include only one untried recipe or lengthy preparation, making the other courses a little easier.

Other aspects of menu planning may seem obvious, but it's worth taking a few minutes to make sure you have a variety of colours, flavours and textures. Choose accompanying salads, vegetables, sauces and garnishes to add contrast where needed.

Here are some menu suggestions using combinations of recipes featured in the book. Plan ahead, allow time to give them your best shot and enjoy them!

MENU SUGGESTIONS

ORIGINAL SUNDAY TIMES MENU
£1 for 4
Spicy Mexican Barbecue Bean Soup
Hot Dog Fusilli
Cinnamon Baked Apples 'en papillote'

ITALIAN VERVE
£4 for 4
Verdura Tonnato
Turkey Osso Buco
Coffee Risotto

SOUTH AMERICAN FEEL
£4 for 4
Ceviche of Whiting
Grilled Chicken Wings
on Drunken Black beans
with Chilli Verde

ENGLISH FARE
£4 for 4
B.L.T. Salad
Soft Roe Potato Cakes
with Caper Mayo
Apple Bread and Butter pudding

GREEK FLAVOURS
£1 for 4
Avgolemono
(Egg and Lemon Soup)
Lentil Moussaka Tart

SUMMER PICNIC
£3 for 4
Arrancini
Verdura Tonnato
Caraway, Onion and Bacon Tart

MEDITERRANEAN INSPIRED
£4 for 4
Sambusak
(Cheese and Potato Pasties)
Cod Tagine

HOT AND COLD PASTA BUFFET
£3 for 4
Jumbled Pasta, Chickpea and
Basil Salad
Spaghetti with Potatoes and Wilted
Beans
Trenette with Tuna and Tomatoes

DINNER IN AN HOUR OR LESS
£4 for 4
Pesto Baked Mushrooms
Grey Mullet in Acqua Pazza
Prune and Almond Frittata

SUMMER EVENING BARBECUE
£4 for 4
Chargrilled Calamari Salad
Persian Koftas with Pitta Toasts
Shanghai Fishburgers
Barbecue Spice Rub Chicken

SOUPS

Pumpkin bisque

Pumpkins are often underrated, but their mellow flavour makes them incredibly versatile, ideal for both sweet and savoury dishes. It's certainly worth making the most of them when they appear in markets in the autumn.

Instead of the bread and garlic in this recipe, you could use six to eight pieces of garlic bread.

25 g (1 oz) butter
1 small onion, chopped
450 g (1 lb) peeled pumpkin, seeds removed, cut into chunks
375 ml (12 fl oz) milk
375 ml (12 fl oz) chicken or vegetable stock
3 slices of white bread
2 garlic cloves, halved
salt and freshly ground pepper
freshly grated nutmeg

Heat the butter in a heavy-bottomed saucepan, add the onion and cook until soft and translucent. Add the pumpkin and cook, stirring occasionally, for a further 5 minutes. Add the milk and stock and bring to the boil.

Meanwhile, lightly toast the bread, then rub with the cut cloves of garlic and cut each slice into four pieces. Add to the boiling soup and reduce the heat to a simmer. Cook for about 30 minutes or until the pumpkin is tender.

Pour into a liquidizer and blend to a fine, creamy-textured purée. If the soup is too thick you may need to add a little more milk. Season to taste with salt, pepper and nutmeg; serve hot.

Mussel chowder

Chowders are normally associated with clams, but I find them tough and tasteless – give me mussels any day. If you are feeling extravagant, add a pinch of saffron to the chowder with the milk and cream; its flavour goes beautifully with mussels.

900 g (2 lb) fresh mussels, scrubbed and debearded
15 g (½ oz) butter
50 g (2 oz) streaky bacon, cut into small pieces
1 onion, chopped
½ leek, cut into small dice
1 carrot, cut into small dice
1 garlic clove, crushed
225 g (8 oz) potatoes, cut into small dice
150 ml (¼ pint) milk
4 tablespoons single cream
chopped fresh parsley
salt and freshly ground pepper

Place the mussels in a large saucepan, add 450 ml ($^{3}/_{4}$ pint) water, cover with a tight-fitting lid and bring to the boil over a high heat. Cook for 2 minutes or until the mussels open. Drain them in a colander, retaining the cooking liquid. Remove the mussels from their shells; discard the shells.

Heat the butter in a heavy-bottomed saucepan, add the bacon, onion, leek, carrot and garlic and cook for 2 minutes or until the vegetables are tender. Strain the mussel cooking liquid and add to the pan, then add the potatoes. Bring to the boil, then reduce the heat and simmer until the potatoes are cooked.

Add the milk and cream, chopped parsley and mussels. Season to taste with pepper and salt if required; serve hot.

Avgolemono
(Greek egg and lemon soup)

I discovered this soup while on holiday in Corfu. I loved its simplicity and tanginess and couldn't wait to try making it myself. Basmati rice, while not authentic, adds a lovely fragrance to the soup. I sometimes serve it lightly chilled.

1 litre (1¾ pints) chicken stock
50 g (2 oz) long-grain rice (preferably basmati)
2 eggs
2 tablespoons fresh lemon juice
salt and freshly ground pepper

Bring the stock to the boil in a saucepan, add the rice and simmer until the rice is cooked and tender, about 12 minutes.

Break the eggs into a bowl, add the lemon juice and whisk until light and frothy.

A little at a time, stir the cooked rice and hot liquid into the eggs, until all is blended together. Return to the pan and cook over a low heat, stirring all the time, until the soup thickens enough to coat the back of a spoon – it must not be allowed to boil. Season to taste with salt and pepper and serve at once. Alternatively, leave to cool, then chill.

Roasted corn broth
with chunky pea guacamole

3 fresh or frozen corn on the cob
50 g (2 oz) butter, melted
salt and freshly ground pepper
750 ml (1¼ pints) chicken or vegetable stock
100 g (4 oz) cooked black beans
50 g (2 oz) Cheddar cheese, coarsely grated

For the pea guacamole:
100 g (4 oz) cooked peas
1 small green chilli, halved, deseeded and finely chopped
2 tomatoes, deseeded and cut into small pieces
2 tablespoons chopped fresh coriander
2 tablespoons shredded spring onions
1 teaspoon fresh lime juice
pinch of ground cumin

Preheat the oven to 200°C/400°F/Gas Mark 6.
Place the corn cobs on a baking sheet, brush with the butter, sprinkle with salt and pepper and cook until tender and lightly browned; this will take 20–25 minutes. Turn the cobs regularly so they brown evenly.

Remove from the oven and, when cool enough to handle, hold the cobs over a chopping board and use a knife to scrape off all the kernels; reserve the kernels. Cut the cobs into chunks and return to the oven to roast for a further 10 minutes.

Bring the stock to the boil in a saucepan, add the roasted cobs, reduce the heat and simmer for 40–45 minutes. Strain the corn broth through a sieve and season to taste.

To make the pea guacamole, mash the peas with a fork, add the remaining ingredients and season to taste.

To serve, divide the guacamole between four soup plates or bowls, add the reserved corn kernels and the black beans, then pour over the broth and top with the grated cheese; serve at once.

Green tomato gazpacho

At the end of summer, gardeners often find they have a glut of green tomatoes. This chilled soup is a great way to use them up, and of course it is just as good with red tomatoes. I like to serve gazpacho topped with a spoonful of crème fraîche mixed with a little shredded fresh basil.

2 slices of white bread, crusts removed
450 g (1 lb) green tomatoes, roughly chopped
1 green pepper, halved, deseeded and roughly chopped
½ cucumber, cut into chunks
½ onion, roughly chopped
1 garlic clove, crushed
½ teaspoon coriander seeds, crushed
5 tablespoons olive oil
4 tablespoons white wine vinegar
salt and freshly ground pepper
sugar

Place the bread in a small bowl and pour on about 600 ml (1 pint) cold water.

Place the tomatoes, pepper, cucumber, onion, garlic and coriander in a liquidizer and blend to a smooth purée. Strain the purée through a fine sieve into a bowl.

Squeeze the water from the bread and place the bread in the liquidizer. Blend to a pulp, then, with the machine running, add the olive oil a little at a time until incorporated into the bread. Add the vinegar, a good pinch of salt and 4 tablespoons of the strained tomato mixture and blend for a further 30 seconds.

Stir the bread mixture into the bowl of tomato mixture. Adjust the consistency by adding a little more water if necessary. Season to taste, adding a pinch of sugar and more vinegar if required. Chill the gazpacho until ready to serve.

Frozen broad bean and lemongrass vichyssoise

This variation on the classic, creamy, chilled vichyssoise has a subtle and delicate flavour; it is just as delicious made with peas instead of broad beans.

75 g (3 oz) butter
75 g (3 oz) leeks, roughly chopped
2 stalks of lemongrass, chopped
½ teaspoon fresh root ginger, chopped
1 litre (1¾ pints) chicken or vegetable stock
450 g (1 lb) frozen broad beans, shelled
250 ml (8 fl oz) milk
salt and freshly ground pepper
sugar
4 sprigs of mint, finely shredded

Heat the butter in a saucepan, add the leeks, lemongrass and ginger and cook over a low heat until soft. Add the stock, bring to the boil and simmer for 10 minutes. Add the shelled beans, return to the boil, then remove from the heat.

Pour into a liquidizer and blend to a purée. (For a really smooth soup, strain through a sieve.) Add the milk and season to taste with salt, pepper and a pinch of sugar. Chill until ready to serve. Sprinkle with the shredded mint just before serving.

Cabbage, turnip
and black pudding soup

1 Savoy cabbage
2 large turnips
4 tablespoons olive oil
1 garlic clove, crushed
1 litre (1¾ pints) chicken stock
100 g (4 oz) black pudding, thinly sliced
salt and freshly ground black pepper

Remove and discard the outside leaves of the cabbage, then cut the cabbage into about 2.5 cm (1 inch) pieces. Peel the turnips and cut them in half, then into 5 mm (¼ inch) thick slices.

Heat half the oil in a large saucepan, add the garlic and cabbage and cook until the cabbage starts to soften. Add the sliced turnips, season lightly and cook for a further 2–3 minutes. Pour in the stock, bring to the boil, reduce the heat and simmer for 20–25 minutes or until the turnips are tender.

Add the black pudding, season to taste and simmer gently for a further 2 minutes. Serve hot, in bowls, drizzled with the remaining olive oil and sprinkled with some coarsely ground black pepper, accompanied by crusty baguette.

French onion soup
with herring crostini

A classic warming soup with a fishy twist!

2 tablespoons olive oil
50 g (2 oz) butter
450 g (1 lb) onions, thinly sliced
2 teaspoons sugar
1 small garlic clove, crushed
1 tablespoon tomato purée
125 ml (4 fl oz) white wine
1 litre (1¾ pints) chicken stock

For the herring crostini:
200 g (7 oz) canned herrings in oil
salt and freshly ground pepper
75 g (3 oz) Cheddar or Gruyère cheese, grated
1 small baguette

Heat the oil and butter in a large saucepan, add the onions and sauté until tender. Sprinkle with the sugar and continue to cook until the sugar caramelizes and the onions turn a beautiful dark brown.

Add the garlic and tomato purée and cook, stirring once or twice, for a further 5 minutes. Pour in the wine and stock, bring to the boil, reduce the heat and simmer for 30–35 minutes.

To make the herring crostini, mash the herrings in a bowl and season lightly. Cut the baguette into eight 1 cm (½ inch) slices, toast them and spread with the mashed herring. Keep warm. Preheat the grill to its highest setting.

Pour the hot soup into heatproof bowls, top each with two herring crostini and sprinkle with the cheese. Place the bowls under the hot grill until the cheese is brown and bubbling. Serve at once.

STARTERS AND SALADS

Pesto baked mushrooms

This stuffing can also be used for tomatoes, courgettes, aubergines or onions, although they will take longer to cook (15–20 minutes for courgettes and 45–55 minutes for aubergines and onions).

450 g (1 lb) large button mushrooms
3 tablespoons olive oil
1 onion, chopped
2 courgettes, chopped
1 small jar of pesto sauce, about 125 ml (4 fl oz)
25–50 g (1–2 oz) Parmesan cheese, grated
1 egg yolk
salt and freshly ground pepper

Gently pull out the stalks from the mushrooms and chop the stalks finely. Heat half the oil in a frying pan, add the chopped onion, courgettes and mushroom stalks and cook over a low heat until soft, about 5 minutes. Leave until cold.

Preheat the oven to 200°C/400°F/Gas Mark 6.

Place the onion mixture in a liquidizer with the pesto sauce and blend to a coarse purée. Add enough Parmesan to form a thick paste. Transfer to a bowl and stir in the egg yolk. Taste and adjust the seasoning.

Lightly fry the mushroom caps in the remaining oil for 1 minute, then drain. Fill each cap with the pesto stuffing, place on a baking sheet and bake for 5–8 minutes or until tender when tested with a small sharp knife. Alternatively, cook the mushrooms under a hot grill. Serve hot.

Oriental mushroom fritters with peanut curry dip

vegetable oil for deep-frying
450 g (1 lb) button mushrooms
2 tablespoons five-spice powder
½ teaspoon dried chilli flakes
150 g (5 oz) cornflour
½ teaspoon baking powder
salt and freshly ground black pepper
1 egg white

For the peanut curry dip:
150 ml (¼ pint) chicken or vegetable stock
½ teaspoon curry powder
½ garlic clove, crushed
½ teaspoon honey
2 tablespoons peanut butter
½ teaspoon light soy sauce
dash of wine vinegar

Heat 2 tablespoons of the oil in a frying pan and fry the mushrooms for 2 minutes or until they begin to soften. Season with five-spice powder and chilli flakes, transfer to a bowl and leave until cold.

To make the peanut curry dip, place all the ingredients in a saucepan and bring to the boil; simmer gently for 3–4 minutes, then leave to cool.

Place the cornflour and baking powder in a bowl with 125 ml (4 fl oz) iced water, 3 tablespoons of the oil and a little salt and pepper and mix until smooth. When you are ready to fry the mushrooms, whisk the egg white until stiff, then fold into the batter.

Heat the oil for deep-frying to 180°C/350°F (until a cube of bread browns in 30 seconds). Dip the mushrooms in the batter, then into the hot oil and fry until golden, 1–2 minutes. Drain well and serve with the peanut dip.

Mexican dirty rice salad

A substantial salad that can equally well be served as a
vegetarian main course, especially with plenty of Mexican
garnishes; diced avocado and tomato, sour cream and
coarsely grated Cheddar cheese.

50 g (2 oz) butter
225 g (8 oz) long-grain rice
1 green chilli, deseeded and chopped
1 teaspoon ground cumin
500 ml (16 fl oz) vegetable stock
salt and freshly ground pepper
400 g (14 oz) canned black beans
4 spring onions, shredded
2 tablespoons chopped fresh coriander

For the dressing:
5 tablespoons vegetable oil
1½ tablespoons white wine vinegar
1 teaspoon mustard

Heat the butter in a wide saucepan over a low heat, add the rice
and cook, stirring, until opaque. Add the chilli and cumin, stir well
and cook for a further 1 minute.

Bring the stock to the boil, add to the rice with 1 teaspoon salt
and bring back to the boil. Reduce the heat, cover with a tight-
fitting lid and cook for 20 minutes or until the rice is tender.

Drain the rice and transfer to a large bowl. Add the black
beans, shredded spring onions and coriander and mix well. Leave
to cool slightly.

Place the dressing ingredients in a bowl and whisk together,
then pour over the rice salad and serve at room temperature.

Crispy Malaysian vegetable salad

150 g (5 oz) broccoli, cut into small florets
2 carrots, cut into matchsticks
½ red pepper, deseeded and cut into matchsticks
½ yellow pepper, deseeded and cut into matchsticks
½ cucumber, cut into matchsticks
50 g (2 oz) beansprouts
4 spring onions, shredded
½ bunch of watercress
2 tablespoons roasted peanuts

For the dressing:
3 tablespoons lime juice
1 tablespoon chopped fresh mint
1 tablespoon chopped fresh coriander
pinch of dried chilli flakes
2 tablespoons light soy sauce
2 tablespoons sugar
6 tablespoons vegetable oil

Place all the dressing ingredients in a bowl and whisk together. This
can be made up to 2 days ahead and kept in the refrigerator.

Blanch the broccoli in boiling salted water until just tender but
retaining a little crunchiness. Rinse under cold water, drain and dry
on paper towels.

Place all the vegetables in a bowl, add the watercress and the
dressing, mix well and leave for up to 15 minutes before serving,
sprinkled with the roasted peanuts.

Baked tomatoes with coddled eggs

4 large beefsteak tomatoes
salt and freshly ground pepper
4 eggs
40 g (1½ oz) butter

Preheat the oven to 160°C/325°F/Gas Mark 3.

Slice the tops off the tomatoes and scoop out the cores, seeds and juice. Sprinkle a little salt and pepper inside the tomato shells, then place them in a lightly buttered ovenproof dish.

Break each egg into a cup, then slide into the tomato shells. Place a little knob of butter on each egg and season with a little more salt and pepper.

Bake the tomatoes for 12–15 minutes or until the egg whites are firm but the yolks are still soft.

Serve hot, topped with a spoonful of tapenade, pesto or chilli verde (page 74).

Thai chicken wings in spiced coconut milk

1 teaspoon curry paste
1 small garlic clove, crushed
¼ teaspoon dried chilli flakes
½ teaspoon ground coriander
½ teaspoon turmeric
salt and freshly ground pepper
sugar
250 ml (8 fl oz) coconut milk
3 tablespoons vegetable oil
20 fresh chicken wings, boned

Place the curry paste, garlic, chilli, spices, salt, pepper and a pinch of sugar in a bowl, add the coconut milk and oil and whisk together. Add the chicken wings and turn to coat them in the marinade. Cover and place in the refrigerator for up to 24 hours.

To serve, soak four or more bamboo skewers in cold water for 30 minutes. Preheat the grill or barbecue. Remove the chicken wings from the marinade and thread them on to the soaked skewers. Grill or barbecue until cooked and golden, turning occasionally; about 5–8 minutes.

I like to serve them with basmati rice, a crisp salad and a dip made from 100 g (4 oz) mayonnaise mixed with 2 tablespoons chopped mango chutney. They are also very good on their own, as cocktail nibbles, or you can use them in the Thai chicken broth (page 33).

Salad of sardines 'Monégasque'

The name comes from a Provençal word for Monaco, and this salad is full of the distinctive ingredients of the south of France; whenever I prepare it I dream of travelling through Provence, stopping for a light lunch and a glass of wine.

175 g (6 oz) new potatoes
100 g (4 oz) dried penne pasta
2 tomatoes, cut into quarters
2 hard-boiled eggs, shelled
½ small onion, cut into rings
4 red radishes
1 teaspoon capers, drained
200 g (7 oz) canned sardines

For the dressing:
2 teaspoons white wine vinegar
6 teaspoons olive oil
½ teaspoon anchovy essence
½ garlic clove, crushed
salt and freshly ground pepper

Boil the potatoes in salted water. At the same time cook the pasta in plenty of boiling salted water, to which a little oil has been added to prevent the pasta from sticking together.

When the potatoes are tender, drain, peel and slice them into a bowl. When the pasta is cooked al dente (just tender, but still firm to the bite), drain in a colander and add to the potatoes. Add the tomatoes, eggs, onion rings, radishes and capers and toss gently.

Drain the sardines, reserving the oil. Place the dressing ingredients in a bowl and whisk together with the sardine oil. Season to taste, then add to the salad and toss gently to mix.

Serve the salad on a serving platter, topped with the sardines. I like to garnish this dish with crunchy deep-fried parsley.

B.L.T. salad (Bacon, liver and tomato salad)

My version of the infamous B.L.T. (normally a sandwich made with bacon, lettuce and tomatoes). My ingredients are bacon, chicken livers and tomatoes, transformed into a delicious warm salad.

6 tablespoons olive oil
400 g (14 oz) fresh chicken livers, cleaned and halved
½ teaspoon ground cumin
6 tomatoes, halved
4 rashers of streaky bacon
2 tablespoons roughly chopped fresh coriander leaves
6 tablespoons balsamic vinegar
mixed salad leaves

Heat half the oil in a frying pan until very hot, add the chicken livers, seasoned with a little cumin, and cook for 2–3 minutes, stirring occasionally, until brown and crisp on the outside, yet still pink and tender inside.

Preheat the grill. Brush the tomatoes with a little olive oil. Grill the bacon and tomatoes until the bacon is crisp and the tomatoes are soft but not mushy. Sprinkle the tomatoes with some of the coriander and keep the bacon and tomatoes warm.

Remove the livers from the frying pan and keep warm. Add the vinegar to the pan and bring to the boil. Whisk in the remaining olive oil.

Toss the salad leaves with some of the warm dressing and arrange on four plates. Crumble the crispy bacon over the leaves and place three tomato halves on each plate. Top with the chicken livers and drizzle the remaining dressing over the livers. Garnish with the remaining coriander leaves.

Asian spiced herrings with fruit raita

1 teaspoon dried chilli flakes
½ garlic clove, crushed
1 teaspoon ground ginger
1 teaspoon garam masala
salt and freshly ground black pepper
6 tablespoons vegetable or olive oil
450 g (1 lb) fresh herrings, cleaned and cut into 5 cm (2 inch) pieces

For the raita sauce:
150 ml (¼ pint) natural yoghurt
½ teaspoon ground cumin
2 teaspoons chopped fresh coriander or mint
1 firm banana

In a shallow dish, mix together the chilli, garlic, ginger, garam masala, salt and pepper. Add 2 tablespoons of the oil and mix to a paste. Add the fish pieces and leave to marinate for 30 minutes.

To make the raita, mix together the yoghurt, cumin and coriander or mint in a bowl. Coarsely grate the banana into the yoghurt, stir gently to mix and season to taste.

Heat the remaining 4 tablespoons oil in a frying pan and fry the herring pieces until golden, about 4 minutes on each side. Drain on paper towels and serve hot, accompanied by the raita.

Ceviche of whiting

In some parts of South America oranges are used instead of limes.

450 g (1 lb) very fresh whiting fillet
juice of 2 limes
salt
1 tablespoon coriander seeds, crushed
4 tablespoons olive oil
½ tablespoon tomato ketchup
dash of Tobasco sauce
1 small onion, finely sliced
2 tomatoes, skinned, deseeded and cut into small dice
50 g (2 oz) cucumber, peeled and cut into small dice
1 tablespoon chopped fresh coriander, plus extra to garnish
corn tortillas, fried until crisp

Cut the fish into 2 cm (¾ inch) cubes and place in a bowl. Pour on the lime juice and a little salt and toss well to coat the fish. Cover the bowl and place it in the refrigerator for up to 5 hours, stirring from time to time. The fish will become opaque.

Drain off the juice and combine some of it (according to taste – you may not need all of it) with the crushed coriander seeds, oil, ketchup and Tobasco to form a dressing. Pour the dressing over the fish and gently stir in the onion, tomatoes, cucumber and fresh coriander. Refrigerate for a further 1 hour.

Serve chilled, layered between the tortilla crisps. Garnish with fresh coriander.

Arrancini

Arrancini is the Italian term for small oranges; these look-alikes are made of red salmon bound with cooked rice and fried until crisp. The traditional accompaniment is a well-flavoured tomato sauce. Tartare sauce or a pesto-flavoured mayonnaise are also good.

200 g (7 oz) arborio rice
1 hard-boiled egg, chopped
200 g (7 oz) canned red salmon, drained and flaked
1 teaspoon chopped fresh parsley
½ teaspoon dried or fresh oregano
salt and freshly ground pepper
1 egg, beaten
150 g (5 oz) fresh white breadcrumbs
vegetable oil for deep-frying
lemon wedges, to serve

Cook the rice in plenty of salted boiling water for 12–15 minutes or until just tender. Drain well and leave to dry for at least 30 minutes. (The rice can be cooked up to a day ahead and kept in the refrigerator.)

Place the cooked rice in a bowl, add the chopped hard-boiled egg, the flaked salmon, herbs, salt and pepper. Place in the refrigerator for 1 hour.

Shape the chilled mixture into tiny balls, about 4 cm (1½ inches) in diameter. Place the beaten egg in a saucer and the breadcrumbs on a plate. Roll the rice balls first in the beaten egg, then in the breadcrumbs.

Heat the oil for deep-frying to 180°C/350°F (until a cube of bread browns in 30 seconds). Fry the rice balls for 3–4 minutes or until golden. Drain on paper towels and serve with lemon wedges.

Tatin of sardines

450 g (1 lb) puff pastry
25 g (1 oz) butter
2 onions, thinly sliced
3 anchovy fillets, finely chopped
600 g (1¼ lb) fresh sardines, filleted, central bones removed
salt and freshly ground pepper
100 ml (3½ fl oz) olive oil
½ garlic clove, crushed
½ teaspoon coriander seeds, crushed
3 tomatoes, deseeded and diced
juice of ½ lemon

Preheat the oven to 200°C/400°F/Gas Mark 6.

Roll out the pastry on a lightly floured board to approximately 5 mm (¼ inch) thick. Using a 10 cm (4 inch) round cutter, cut out four pastry circles, prick each thoroughly with a fork and bake for 8–10 minutes or until cooked and golden. Remove from the oven and leave to cool.

Meanwhile, heat the butter in a saucepan, add the sliced onions and cook gently until golden, then add the chopped anchovies. Spread each baked tart with the onion and anchovy mixture. Arrange the sardine fillets on top. Season and brush with a little of the olive oil. Place in a hot oven for 5–6 minutes or until the sardines are cooked and lightly browned.

While the tarts are cooking, prepare a light sauce: heat the remaining oil in a saucepan, add the garlic and coriander seeds and heat gently. Add the diced tomatoes, lemon juice and salt and pepper and warm through to soften the tomatoes. Pour the sauce around the tarts and serve hot.

Chargrilled calamari salad

However you cook them, squid need a very short cooking time, otherwise they will toughen. If you want to cook them on the barbecue, leave them whole and cut them into rings when cooked. If you prefer your squid to be crispy, dip the rings in breadcrumbs and deep-fry until golden. There are several good brands of frozen squid (calamari) at very reasonable prices.

4 tomatoes, cut into quarters
6 black olives, pitted and halved
1 red onion, halved and thinly sliced
1 tablespoon fresh oregano leaves
600 g (1¼ lb) squid, cleaned and cut into 5 mm (¼ inch) rings
salt and freshly ground pepper
2 Little Gem lettuces, or other crisp lettuce leaves

For the sauce:
2 garlic cloves, crushed
4 tablespoons olive oil
4 tablespoons vegetable oil
1 egg
1 tablespoon white wine vinegar
dash of Worcestershire sauce
dash of Tobasco sauce

To make the sauce, whisk all the ingredients together in a bowl or blend in a liquidizer.

Toss the tomatoes, olives, onion and oregano together with just enough of the sauce to coat lightly.

Sprinkle the squid with a little salt and pepper and grill for 1 minute under a hot grill or in a cast-iron grill pan.

Arrange the lettuce leaves on four plates, top with the tomato salad, then the grilled squid; serve warm.

Beetroot 'gravad mackerel'

Mackerel makes an interesting variation on the classic Scandinavian gravadlax (marinated salmon). Beetroot has a sweet taste that goes well with the sweet dill and mustard sauce.

2 tablespoons sugar
3 tablespoons salt
a little freshly ground pepper
4 large, very fresh mackerel, cleaned and filleted
5 tablespoons chopped fresh dill, plus extra to garnish
1 cooked fresh beetroot (not in vinegar), coarsely grated
1 tablespoon capers (optional), to garnish
lemon wedges, to serve

For the sauce:
2 tablespoons mustard
2 teaspoons brown sugar
1 tablespoon white wine vinegar
4 tablespoons olive oil
2 tablespoons chopped fresh dill

Mix the sugar, salt and pepper together in a bowl. Lay the mackerel fillets out flat, skin side down, and sprinkle with the sugar and salt mixture. Cover each fillet with some of the chopped dill. Arrange the fillets head to tail in a shallow dish, just large enough to hold the fish. Sprinkle with the remaining dill, then cover with clingfilm and press down with a weighted board, about 1–1.5 kg (2–3 lb). Leave in the refrigerator for 8 hours.

Sprinkle the grated beetroot over the fish and return to the refrigerator for a further 8 hours.

To make the sauce, mix the mustard, sugar and vinegar together in a bowl, whisk in the oil, add the dill and season to taste.

To serve, scrape the dill mixture and beetroot from the fish and, using a long, sharp knife, cut the fillets into thin slices, beginning at the tail end.

Garnish with fresh dill and capers, if using. Serve with lemon wedges and serve the sauce separately.

Soft roe potato cakes with caper mayo

225 g (8 oz) soft herring roes, cleaned
75 ml (3 fl oz) milk
40 g (1½ oz) butter, softened
1 onion, finely chopped
275 g (10 oz) cooked mashed potatoes
1 teaspoon chopped fresh parsley
salt and freshly ground pepper
freshly grated nutmeg
2 large potatoes
3–4 tablespoons plain flour
2 eggs, beaten
vegetable oil for frying

For the caper mayo:
100 g (4 oz) mayonnaise
1 tablespoon chopped capers
juice and grated zest of 1 lemon

Poach the roes in the milk for 6–8 minutes, then drain, discarding the milk, and leave to cool.

Heat half the butter in a frying pan, add the onion and cook until golden. Place the mashed potatoes in a bowl, add the onion and beat in the remaining butter until smooth. Dice the cooked roes and gently stir into the potatoes, together with the parsley. Season to taste with salt, pepper and nutmeg. Place in the refrigerator for 1 hour.

Mix the ingredients for the caper mayonnaise in a small bowl.

Peel and grate the potatoes, and dry them in a clean tea towel. Divide the mashed potato mixture into eight pieces, then shape into ovals. Dip the potato cakes into the flour to coat lightly, then coat them with the beaten eggs, then finally coat them evenly with the grated potatoes.

Heat the oil in a frying pan and cook the potato cakes until golden and crisp on both sides, about 3–4 minutes. Drain on paper towels and serve hot, with the caper mayonnaise.

Roes on toast

Soft roes, for me, are one of our greatest treasures at a budget price, but unfortunately they are seldom used. Try them simply on toast, for breakfast or brunch, and you will discover just what you have been missing. Malt vinegar is the traditional dressing.

50 g (2 oz) butter
400 g (14 oz) soft herring roes, cleaned
salt and freshly ground black pepper
4 slices of white bread
2 tablespoons malt vinegar

Heat the butter in a frying pan, season the roes with salt and pepper and fry them until they begin to curl up and turn golden, about 1–2 minutes.

Meanwhile, toast the bread.

Arrange the roes on the toast and serve at once, sprinkled with the vinegar and a generous amount of black pepper.

Thai mussels

Mussels are often served as a first course in restaurants, but because they are quite fiddly to eat, they are very filling, and can easily become the main event.

900 g (2 lb) fresh mussels, scrubbed and debearded
2 tablespoons vegetable oil
½ onion, finely chopped
2 fresh red chillies, deseeded and finely chopped
(or ½ teaspoon dried chilli flakes)
2 small garlic cloves, crushed
½ tablespoon brown sugar
1 tablespoon light soy sauce
2 tablespoons roughly chopped fresh mint
freshly ground black pepper

Place the mussels in a frying pan or a fairly shallow saucepan. Pour over 150 ml (¼ pint) water, cover with a tight-fitting lid and place over a high heat until the shells open, about 2–3 minutes. Transfer the mussels to a serving dish.

Heat the oil in the cleaned frying pan, add the onion, chillies, garlic, sugar and soy sauce and cook until tender. Pour the mixture over the mussels, sprinkle with the chopped mint and pepper and serve at once.

Grilled stuffed mussels with pico de gallo

Pico de gallo means 'chicken's beak' in Spanish, and is the name given to a piquant salsa. You could add more Tobasco sauce to heighten the flavour, but take care not to overwhelm the mussels.

900 g (2 lb) fresh mussels, scrubbed and debearded
5 tablespoons white wine
25 g (1 oz) fresh white breadcrumbs
salt and freshly ground pepper

For the pico de gallo:
200 g (7 oz) canned tomatoes, drained and finely chopped
½ onion
½ garlic clove, crushed
½ teaspoon coriander seeds, crushed
1 tablespoon fresh coriander
2 tablespoons lime juice
1 tablespoon maple syrup
5 tablespoons olive oil
2 drops of Tobasco sauce

Place the mussels in a frying pan or a fairly shallow saucepan. Add the white wine and 125 ml (4 fl oz) water, cover with a tight-fitting lid and place over a high heat until the shells open, about 2–3 minutes. Drain the mussels in a colander, strain the cooking liquid and set aside.

Remove the mussels from their shells and discard the shells that have the inner muscle attached. Arrange the mussels in their half shells on a baking sheet.

Make the pico de gallo by placing all the ingredients in a liquidizer or food processor and blending together. Pour the mixture into a bowl, add the breadcrumbs and season lightly.

Place a little of the pico de gallo stuffing on each mussel half and cook under a preheated hot grill until golden and crisp.

Place a little of the reserved mussel cooking liquid in the bottom of each serving bowl and top with the grilled mussels; serve at once.

PASTA AND Co.

Penne with caramelized celery, walnut and sage gremolata

This is a delicious dish for vegetarians – but it is also very good with the addition of 50 g (2 oz) of sautéed bacon.

75 g (3 oz) butter
225 g (8 oz) celery, thinly sliced
1 teaspoon sugar
4 tablespoons red wine
1 tablespoon balsamic vinegar
2 tablespoons olive oil
450 g (1 lb) penne pasta
salt and freshly ground pepper
freshly grated nutmeg

For the gremolata:
50 g (2 oz) walnuts
75 g (3 oz) fresh white breadcrumbs
½ garlic clove, crushed
1 tablespoon chopped fresh sage

Heat 25 g (1 oz) of the butter in a frying pan, add the celery and sugar and cook until soft and lightly golden. Pour in the wine and vinegar and continue cooking to form a lightly caramelized glaze around the celery.

Place all the ingredients for the gremolata in a liquidizer and blend together.

Heat the remaining butter in a frying pan with the olive oil, add the gremolata and cook until golden and crunchy.

Cook the pasta in boiling salted water until al dente (just tender, but still firm to the bite). Drain and mix with the caramelized celery. Taste and adjust the seasoning and serve hot, sprinkled with the gremolata.

Fettucine with charred tomatoes and rosemary oil

If you know someone who owns a rosemary bush, you have a supply of fresh rosemary all year round. This hardy herb is not just for use with lamb. Here it makes a tasty oil for a simple pasta dish.

450 g (1 lb) small plum tomatoes, halved
1 garlic clove, crushed
1 tablespoon sugar
salt and freshly ground pepper
450 g (1 lb) fettucine pasta
6 tablespoons olive oil
40 g (1½ oz) fresh rosemary
freshly grated nutmeg

Preheat the oven to 200°C/400°F/Gas Mark 6.

Place the halved tomatoes on a lightly greased baking sheet, rub each with half of the garlic, then sprinkle with sugar and a little salt and pepper. Bake the tomatoes for 10–15 minutes or until soft and slightly charred. Alternatively, place them under a hot grill to achieve the same result.

Cook the fettucine in boiling salted water al dente (just tender, but still firm to the bite), then drain.

Place the olive oil, rosemary and remaining garlic in a liquidizer and blend to a purée. Season to taste. Toss the pasta with the rosemary oil and adjust the seasoning with salt, pepper and nutmeg. Top with the charred tomatoes and serve at once.

Rigatoni with white bean hummus

450 g (1 lb) rigatoni pasta
6 tablespoons olive oil
4 tablespoons chopped fresh parsley
150 ml (¼ pint) White Bean Hummus (page 42)
salt and freshly ground black pepper

Cook the pasta in boiling salted water until al dente (just tender, but still firm to the bite). Drain the pasta, retaining a little of the cooking water.

Return the pasta to the pan, add the olive oil and parsley, then carefully stir in the white bean hummus and a little of the cooking water to form a sauce around the pasta. Season with salt and a good sprinkling of freshly ground black pepper and serve hot.

Parsley mash gnocchi with blue cheese

900 g (2 lb) potatoes (Cara or Maris Piper), peeled
salt and freshly ground pepper
275 g (10 oz) plain flour
1 egg
freshly grated nutmeg
25 g (1 oz) fresh parsley, chopped

For the blue cheese sauce:
150 g (5 oz) cold butter, cut into small pieces
100 g (4 oz) blue cheese (e.g. Stilton), crumbled

Place the potatoes in a saucepan, cover with water, add a good pinch of salt and bring to the boil. Cook until tender, drain well and then dry in a clean tea towel. Rub the potatoes through a fine sieve into a large bowl. Add the flour, egg, salt, pepper and nutmeg to taste. Mix well together, add the parsley and beat to form a smooth dough.

With floured hands, roll the dough into long, 2 cm (¾ inch) diameter cylinders, then cut into 2 cm (¾ inch) pieces. Using a fork, make an indentation on each piece. Place the gnocchi on a floured tray until ready to cook.

Bring a large saucepan of salted water to the boil, then reduce to a simmer, add the gnocchi and poach gently for 3–4 minutes or until they rise to the surface of the water. Drain them well and keep warm in a buttered serving dish.

To make the sauce, boil 125 ml (4 fl oz) water in a small saucepan, whisk in the pieces of cold butter a few at a time, then whisk in the blue cheese and season to taste. Toss the gnocchi with the sauce and serve at once.

Trenette with tuna and tomatoes

6 tablespoons olive oil
225 g (8 oz) flat mushrooms, cut into small dice
1 tablespoon dried oregano
1 tablespoon chopped fresh parsley
400 g (14 oz) canned tomatoes, drained and roughly chopped
2 tablespoons tomato purée
sugar
185 g (6½ oz) canned tuna, drained and flaked
salt and freshly ground pepper
450 g (1 lb) trenette pasta or spaghettini
freshly grated nutmeg

Heat half the olive oil in a frying pan, add the diced mushrooms and cook over a fairly high heat until lightly golden. Add the oregano and half the parsley.

Add the roughly chopped tomatoes, the tomato purée and a pinch of sugar and cook over a low heat until the sauce thickens. Add the flaked tuna and gently stir into the sauce. Season to taste and stir in the remaining oil. Keep warm.

Cook the pasta in boiling salted water until al dente (just tender, but still firm to the bite). Drain well, return to the pan and season with salt, pepper and nutmeg. Place the pasta in a serving dish and pour over the tuna sauce. Sprinkle with the remaining chopped parsley and serve at once.

Penne with spring vegetables and mint

2 rashers of streaky bacon, cut into small pieces
100 g (4 oz) frozen (or fresh) peas
100 g (4 oz) frozen (or fresh) broad beans, blanched and skinned
100 g (4 oz) young leeks, cut into 5 mm (¼ inch) slices
450 ml (¾ pint) chicken stock
4 tablespoons olive oil
50 g (2 oz) butter
450 g (1 lb) penne pasta
2 tablespoons shredded fresh mint leaves

Heat a heavy-bottomed saucepan, add the bacon and fry until the bacon releases its juices and becomes crisp. Remove from the pan and set aside.

Add the peas, beans and leeks to the pan, cover with the stock and cook until the vegetables are tender. Lift out the vegetables with a slotted spoon and keep warm.

Boil the stock over a high heat until reduced to about 150 ml (¼ pint), then whisk in the oil and butter.

Meanwhile, cook the pasta in boiling water until al dente (just tender, but still firm to the bite). Drain well, then add to the sauce and return the vegetables to the pan, add the mint, toss well together and serve at once, sprinkled with the crisp bacon.

Spaghetti with potatoes and wilted beans

This dish originates from Liguria in Italy. I love the peasanty feel to it – as well as the fact that it's all cooked in one pan and there isn't too much washing up to do!

3 waxy potatoes, cut into 1 cm (½ inch) cubes
150 g (5 oz) trimmed green beans
450 g (1 lb) spaghetti
1 small jar of pesto sauce, about 125 ml (4 fl oz)
2 tablespoons grated Parmesan cheese (optional)

Boil the potatoes in a large saucepan of lightly salted water until tender but still retaining their shape. Using a slotted spoon, transfer the potatoes from the water to a bowl. Add the beans to the same water and boil until fairly well cooked and soft, then remove and add to the potatoes.

Now add the spaghetti to the pan and cook until al dente (just tender, but still firm to the bite). Drain the spaghetti well, retaining 125 ml (4 fl oz) of the cooking liquid.

Mix the reserved cooking liquid with the pesto sauce. Add the spaghetti to the potatoes and beans, together with the sauce, and toss to combine. Taste and adjust the seasoning if required. Serve at once, with grated Parmesan if liked.

Hot dog fusilli

This dish evolved from the original £1 challenge. Frankfurter sausages are sold in cans or vacuum-packed, or you could use standard pork sausages – it's a very versatile recipe.

6 tablespoons olive oil
225 g (8 oz) frankfurter sausages, blanched in boiling water for 3 minutes, chilled and sliced 1 cm (½ inch) thick
1 teaspoon dried sage or mixed herbs
½ garlic clove, crushed
pinch of dried chilli flakes
200 g (7 oz) canned tomatoes, with juice, chopped
salt and freshly ground pepper
450 g (1 lb) fusilli pasta
4 tablespoons grated Parmesan cheese (optional)

Heat 2 tablespoons of the oil in a frying pan, add the sliced sausage and cook until golden. Stir in the herbs, then remove the sausages from the pan and keep warm.

Add a little more oil to the pan, then add the garlic, chilli and tomatoes and cook until the tomatoes have thickened slightly and become separated from the oil. Season to taste and keep warm.

Cook the fusilli in plenty of boiling salted water until al dente (just tender, but still firm to the bite), then drain and return to the pan. Add the tomato sauce and the sausages and toss together. Heat through gently, taste and adjust the seasoning and serve hot.

Open pasta with scrambled eggs and mussels

The idea of pasta with mussels, mint and scrambled egg may sound strange, but try it and you will be surprised how well they work together.

450 g (1 lb) mussels, scrubbed
5 tablespoons white wine
4 tablespoons double cream
1 tablespoon fresh mint, chopped
8 lasagne sheets, fresh or dried
salt and freshly ground pepper
4 eggs, beaten
50 g (2 oz) butter

Place the mussels in a saucepan, add the wine and 150 ml ($^1/_4$ pint) water. Bring to the boil, cover with a lid and cook over a high heat for 2 minutes or until the shells open. Drain the mussels in a colander, reserving the cooking liquid. Leave to cool slightly, then remove the mussels from their shells and remove their beards.

Strain the mussel cooking liquid into a clean pan and boil over a high heat to reduce it to half its original volume. Add the cream and reduce again until the sauce thickens enough to coat the back of a spoon. Strain through a fine sieve and keep warm.

Cook the lasagne in boiling salted water until al dente (just tender, but still firm to the bite), then drain.

Break the eggs into a bowl and whisk them together with a little salt and pepper. Heat the butter in a saucepan, pour in the eggs and cook, stirring, until creamy.

To serve, add the mussels and mint to the sauce. Lay a sheet of pasta on each plate, top with the scrambled egg and coat with the mussel sauce, then top with another pasta sheet. Serve at once.

Linguine with garlic-chilli oil

125ml (4 fl oz) olive oil
salt and freshly ground pepper
450 g (1 lb) linguine pasta
3 garlic cloves, crushed
½ teaspoon dried chilli flakes
1 tablespoon chopped fresh parsley
freshly grated nutmeg

Bring a large saucepan of water to the boil with 2 tablespoons of the oil and a little salt . Add the pasta and cook until al dente (just tender, but still firm to the bite).

Meanwhile, prepare the sauce. Heat the remaining olive oil in a saucepan, add the garlic and chilli flakes and cook over a low heat for 1–2 minutes.

When the pasta is cooked, drain it in a colander, then add it to the garlic and chilli oil, toss together gently, add the parsley and season to taste with salt, pepper and nutmeg. Serve hot.

Crushed sweetcorn risotto with courgettes

100 g (4 oz) butter
½ onion, finely chopped
225 g (8 oz) arborio rice
600 ml (1 pint) chicken stock, hot
150 g (5 oz) frozen or canned sweetcorn
4 tablespoons single cream
75 g (3 oz) courgettes, sliced lengthways into ribbons
2 tablespoons chopped fresh mint
salt and freshly ground pepper

Heat 75 g (3 oz) of the butter in a heavy-bottomed frying pan, add the onion and cook over a low heat until tender. Add the rice and stir well to coat with the butter. Add a little of the stock and stir until the liquid has been absorbed.

Keep adding the stock a little at a time, stirring constantly, until the rice is tender but retains a little bite (about 20–25 minutes). Towards the end of the cooking time, add the stock in smaller quantities and check whether the rice is done. The final consistency should be loose but not sloppy.

Meanwhile, place the sweetcorn and cream in a liquidizer and blend to a coarse purée. Heat the remaining butter in a frying pan, add the courgettes and sauté until tender.

Add the sweetcorn purée to the risotto. Sprinkle the courgettes with the mint and a little salt and pepper and gently stir them into the risotto. Serve at once.

Chicken liver risotto

100 g (4 oz) butter
½ onion, finely chopped
¼ teaspoon dried thyme
225 g (8 oz) arborio rice
3 tablespoons dry white wine
900 ml (1½ pints) chicken stock, hot
3 tablespoons vegetable oil
400 g (14 oz) chicken livers, cleaned and halved
6 tablespoons madeira
150 ml (¼ pint) double cream, lightly whipped

Melt 75 g (3 oz) of the butter in a heavy-bottomed frying pan, add the onion and thyme and cook over a low heat until softened but not browned. Add the rice and stir well to coat with the butter. Cook over a low heat for 2 minutes until the rice becomes opaque.

Increase the heat, pour in the wine and cook for 4–5 minutes or until the wine has evaporated.

Add the stock a little at a time, stirring constantly, adding more as it is absorbed, until about 600 ml (1 pint) of stock has been used and the rice is tender but retains a little bite (about 20–25 minutes).

Heat the oil and the remaining butter in a frying pan, add the chicken livers and cook over a high heat to seal in their juices. Remove from the pan and keep warm. Add the madeira and the remaining 300 ml (½ pint) chicken stock to the pan and boil to reduce to a syrupy consistency.

To finish the risotto, beat in the cream and a little more butter, taste and adjust the seasoning if required. Divide the risotto between four serving dishes, top with the chicken livers and their sauce and serve at once.

MAINCOURSES

Bourride of smoked haddock

50 g (2 oz) butter
½ onion, chopped
1 garlic clove, crushed
100 g (4 oz) leeks, shredded
1 carrot, cut into 5 mm (¼ inch) dice
275 g (10 oz) potatoes, cut into 5 mm (¼ inch) dice
450 ml (¾ pint) fish stock
450 g (1 lb) smoked haddock
6 tablespoons mayonnaise

Heat the butter in a saucepan, add the onion, garlic and leeks and cook over a low heat for 5–8 minutes or until the vegetables are tender. Add the carrot and potato dice and cook for a further 5 minutes. Pour in the stock and bring to the boil, then reduce the heat and simmer for 10 minutes.

Add the smoked haddock and cook for 5 minutes. Using a slotted spoon, remove the haddock and vegetables and keep warm. Flake the fish into fairly large pieces.

Boil the stock over a high heat to reduce it to 250 ml (8 fl oz). Remove from the heat and beat in the mayonnaise. Return to the heat and bring to just below boiling point. Return the flaked fish and vegetables to the sauce and serve hot.

Kedgeree in filo purses

75 g (3 oz) butter
½ onion, chopped
2 teaspoons curry paste
225 g (8 oz) cooked rice (preferably basmati)
250 g (9 oz) smoked haddock, cooked and flaked
3 eggs, hard-boiled and chopped
5 tablespoons double cream
salt and freshly ground black pepper
1 tablespoon chopped fresh coriander
8 sheets of filo pastry, 20 cm (8 inches) square

Heat half the butter in a large saucepan, add the onion and cook over a low heat until tender. Add the curry paste and stir to combine with the onion. Add the rice and mix well, then add the haddock and eggs and stir in gently so that you do not break up the fish. Add the cream, season to taste and transfer to a bowl. When cool, add the coriander and leave in the refrigerator for up to 1 hour.

Preheat the oven to 190°C/375°F/Gas Mark 5.

Melt the remaining butter. Place 4 filo pastry squares on a work surface and brush with a little of the butter. Set another square of filo on top of each one and spoon a quarter of the kedgeree mixture into the centre. Brush the edges of the pastry with a little more butter, then bring the sides up over the filling and pinch together to form purse shapes. Brush the outsides with butter, then bake for 12–15 minutes or until golden. Leave to cool slightly before serving.

Baked plaice with sardine tapenade

Canned sardines can be used if fresh are not available, but the result is not as good.

4 fresh plaice fillets, about 150 g (5 oz) each
salt and freshly ground pepper
8 small fresh sardine fillets, boneless, finely chopped
1 onion, finely chopped
2 tablespoons black olives, finely chopped
1 tablespoon capers, drained and finely chopped
2 tablespoons fresh white breadcrumbs
6 tablespoons olive oil
1 tablespoon maple syrup
1 tablespoon white wine vinegar
3 tablespoons mustard
1 tablespoon chopped chives

Preheat the oven to 190°C/375°F/Gas Mark 5.

Season the plaice fillets with a little salt and pepper. In a bowl, combine the sardines, onion, olives, capers and breadcrumbs. Add salt and pepper with care: you should not need much salt.

Spread the mixture on the plaice fillets, roll up and secure each fillet with a cocktail stick. Place on a baking sheet, spoon a little olive oil over each fillet and bake for 8–10 minutes.

Meanwhile, heat the maple syrup and vinegar together in a small saucepan, then whisk in the mustard, olive oil and chives.

Transfer the cooked plaice fillets to a serving dish and coat with the sauce; serve at once.

Grey mullet in 'acqua pazza'

This dish of mullet in 'crazy water' (acqua pazza) is simplicity itself; I learnt it when we hosted a culinary promotion with the hotel San Pietro from Positano in Italy.

4 fresh grey mullet fillets
2 garlic cloves, thinly sliced
5 tablespoons olive oil
¼ teaspoon dried chilli flakes
400 g (14 oz) canned plum tomatoes, drained and chopped
2 tablespoons chopped fresh parsley
1 teaspoon fresh or dried oregano
1 teaspoon anchovy essence (optional)
salt and freshly ground pepper

Remove all the bones from the grey mullet fillets and set aside.

Place 750 ml (1¼ pints) water in a wide saucepan or deep frying pan and bring to the boil. Add the garlic, olive oil and chilli flakes, reduce the heat and simmer for 10 minutes. Add the tomatoes, herbs and anchovy essence and simmer for a further 25 minutes; the mixture will reduce and thicken.

Season the fish with salt and pepper and add to the pan. Simmer for 10 minutes or until cooked. Serve with steamed potatoes drizzled with olive oil.

Baked cod with tomato and mustard sauce

This simple dish is elevated to gourmet status by serving it on a bed of creamy mashed potato to which you have added a generous spoonful of pesto sauce and a knob of butter. Sautéed courgettes are the ideal accompaniment.

4 fresh cod fillets, about 150 g (5 oz) each, boneless, cleaned
25 g (1 oz) butter
1 onion, finely chopped
1 tablespoon fennel seeds
pinch of mixed herbs
450 g (1 lb) fresh tomatoes, skinned, deseeded and roughly chopped
2 teaspoons English mustard
2 teaspoons brown sugar
salt and freshly ground pepper
pinch of cayenne pepper
1 tablespoon fresh chopped parsley

Preheat the oven to 190°C/375°F/Gas Mark 5. Place the fish in a lightly buttered ovenproof dish.

Heat the butter in a saucepan, add the onion and fry until tender. Add the fennel seeds, herbs, tomatoes, mustard and brown sugar. Mix well, then season to taste with salt, pepper and cayenne.

Pour the sauce over the fish and bake for 20–25 minutes. sprinkle with fresh parsley and serve hot.

Shanghai fishburgers with cumin and ginger ketchup

450 g (1 lb) whiting or other white fish fillet
1 tablespoon finely chopped fresh root ginger
3 spring onions, finely chopped
1 tablespoon chopped fresh coriander
¼ teaspoon dried chilli flakes
1 tablespoon soy sauce
2 eggs, beaten
1 tablespoon cornflour
salt and freshly ground pepper
4 tablespoons vegetable oil
2 baps
lettuce leaves, to serve

For the cumin and ginger ketchup:
6 tablespoons mayonnaise
1 tablespoon tomato ketchup
¼ teaspoon ground cumin
¼ teaspoon chopped fresh root ginger

Feel the fish to check there are no bones left. Mince the fish in a food processor and place in a bowl. Add the ginger, spring onions, coriander, chilli flakes and soy sauce and stir to mix. Bind the mixture with the eggs and cornflour, season lightly, then leave in the refrigerator for 1 hour.

Mix together all the ingredients for the ketchup in a small bowl.

Shape the chilled fish mixture into eight small burgers. Heat the oil in a frying pan and fry the fishburgers gently until golden, about 3–4 minutes on each side. Drain on paper towels.

Meanwhile, slice the baps in half and toast them, top with the lettuce and the hot fishburgers and serve at once, accompanied by the ketchup, and crisp, thin French fries.

Fresh salt cod
on herb-braised potatoes

4 cod fillets, about 150 g (5 oz) each
1 tablespoon salt (preferably sea salt)
75 g (3 oz) butter
1 onion, thinly sliced
freshly ground pepper
450 g (1 lb) large potatoes
50 g (2 oz) selection of fresh herbs (thyme, rosemary, parsley), chopped
300 ml (½ pint) chicken stock, boiling
6 tablespoons olive oil

Place the fish fillets in a shallow dish, sprinkle evenly with the salt and leave overnight in the refrigerator.

The next day, use 25 g (1 oz) of the butter to grease an oven-proof serving dish. Preheat the oven to 190°C/375°F/Gas Mark 5.

Heat 25 g (1 oz) of the butter in a frying pan and fry the onion over a low heat until golden. Season with salt and pepper.

Thinly slice the potatoes and layer them over the base of the buttered dish, season and top with some of the onions; add another layer of potato slices, salt and pepper, more onion, and a final layer of potatoes. Sprinkle on the herbs. Dot the top layer of potatoes with the remaining butter, season with salt and pepper and pour on the boiling stock. Bake for 50 minutes or until tender and golden.

Heat the olive oil in a frying pan. Carefully wash and dry the cod fillets, then fry them in the oil for 1 minute on each side or until golden.

Place the cod fillets on top of the potatoes, season lightly with salt and pepper and return to the oven for a further 8–10 minutes. Serve hot.

Cod tagine

4 cod (or other white fish) fillets, about 150 g (5 oz) each
8 tablespoons vegetable oil
2 tablespoons ground cumin
2 teaspoons turmeric
1 onion, chopped
1 garlic clove, crushed
2 potatoes, cut into 1 cm (½ inch) dice
2 carrots, cut into 1 cm (½ inch) dice
100 g (4 oz) pumpkin, cut into 1 cm (½ inch) dice
1 teaspoon ground ginger
1 teaspoon ground cinnamon
400 g (14 oz) canned cannellini beans
50 g (2 oz) prunes, soaked overnight and stoned

Marinate the cod with 4 tablespoons of the oil, the cumin and turmeric and place in the refrigerator for 1 hour.

Preheat the oven to 200°C/400°F/Gas Mark 6.

Heat the remaining oil in a large saucepan, add the onion and garlic and cook over a low heat until tender. Add the potatoes, carrots and pumpkin and fry until golden, then add the ginger and cinnamon. Reduce the heat and cook gently for 5 minutes.

Add the cannellini beans, prunes and 125 ml (4 fl oz) water and cook until the vegetables are tender. Taste and adjust the seasoning.

Place the fish on a baking sheet, brush with the marinade and bake in the hot oven for 5–8 minutes or until cooked. Serve the fish on a warmed plate, surrounded by the tagine of vegetables and accompanied by couscous.

Grilled mackerel
with sweet and sour rhubarb

Mackerel is classically served with a gooseberry sauce; the point is that it needs a sharp flavour to offset the oiliness of the fish, such as this tangy rhubarb sauce.

4 tablespoons olive oil
200 g (7 oz) canned tomatoes, drained and finely chopped
325 g (12 oz) fresh rhubarb, peeled and cut into small chunks
3 tablespoons brown sugar
2 tablespoons balsamic vinegar
salt and freshly ground pepper
pinch of ground cinnamon
pinch of ground ginger
1 tablespoon chopped fresh coriander
4 fresh mackerel, about 400 g (14 oz) each

Heat half the olive oil in a wide saucepan, add the tomatoes and simmer over a low heat until they become thick and pulpy. Add the rhubarb, brown sugar and vinegar and bring to the boil, then reduce the heat and cook gently for 8–10 minutes or until the sauce is thick. Season to taste with salt, pepper, cinnamon and ginger; you may need to add a little more sugar if the rhubarb is very acidic. Add the fresh coriander to the sauce and keep warm.

Clean the mackerel, remove the fillets and cut three small incisions into the flesh on both sides. Season and brush them with the remaining olive oil. Place under a hot grill and cook for 5–6 minutes on each side or until golden and crisp.

Serve the grilled mackerel with the rhubarb sauce, accompanied by some sautéed aubergine slices.

Braised chicken
with anchovies and olives

8 chicken thighs
8 chicken drumsticks
3 tablespoons olive oil
salt and freshly ground pepper
2 garlic cloves, crushed
150 ml (5 fl oz) white wine
2 tablespoons balsamic vinegar
600 ml (1 pint) chicken stock
75 g (3 oz) pitted black olives
4 anchovy fillets, rinsed to remove excess salt, drained and chopped

Cut three incisions in each of the chicken pieces. Heat the oil in a flameproof casserole, add the seasoned chicken pieces and cook until golden brown all over.

Add the garlic and stir to mix, then pour in the wine and the vinegar and bring to the boil. Add the stock, olives and anchovies. Cover with a lid and simmer gently for 40–45 minutes until the chicken is cooked and tender. Serve with buttery noodles.

Bstila of chicken with sweet spices

75 g (3 oz) butter
2 large chicken breasts
225 g (8 oz) fresh chicken livers
salt and freshly ground pepper
1 small onion, chopped
½ teaspoon garlic, crushed
¼ teaspoon turmeric
¼ teaspoon ground ginger
¼ teaspoon ground cumin
¼ teaspoon ground allspice
a little chicken stock (optional)
1 egg
75 g (3 oz) almonds, toasted
1 teaspoon ground cinnamon, plus extra for dusting
½ teaspoon sugar
100 g (4 oz) cooked rice (preferably basmati)
2 tablespoons chopped fresh coriander or parsley
pinch of cayenne pepper
4 sheets of filo pastry, about 20 cm (8 inches) square
a little egg wash

Preheat the oven to 180°C/350°F/Gas Mark 4.

Heat the butter in a frying pan and fry the lightly seasoned chicken breasts and livers over a high heat until golden. Remove from the pan. Add the onion and garlic to the pan with the turmeric, ginger, cumin and allspice and cook for 1 minute to release their fragrance. Return the chicken breasts to the pan, half cover with stock or water and bring to the boil. Reduce the heat and simmer for 8 minutes. Add the livers and cook for a further 2–3 minutes. Remove the breasts and livers from the pan and cut them into 2 cm (³/₄ inch) dice.

Boil the cooking liquid until it becomes syrupy in consistency. Leave to cool slightly, then whisk in the egg.

In a bowl, mix together the almonds, cinnamon, sugar and cooked rice. Add the fresh herbs and cayenne pepper.

Place two sheets of filo pastry in a baking tin about 20 cm (8 inches) square. Brush with the sauce and egg mixture, then add the diced chicken and livers. Top with the rice mixture, add the remaining sauce, then cover with the remaining filo pastry and tuck down the sides. Brush with egg wash and a light criss-cross dusting of cinnamon. Bake for 15–20 minutes or until golden. Serve hot.

Grilled chicken wings on drunken black beans with chilli verde

Instead of the chicken wings, I also like to make this dish with lambs' kidneys or pork chops.

175 g (6 oz) black turtle beans, picked over and rinsed
1 garlic clove, crushed
1 tablespoon ground cumin
100 ml (3½ fl oz) lager
3 tablespoons olive oil
salt and freshly ground pepper
8 chicken wings

For the chilli verde:
½ green pepper, deseeded
1 green chilli, deseeded
3 tablespoons chopped fresh coriander
3 spring onions, finely chopped
2 tablespoons white wine vinegar
½ teaspoon mustard
3 tablespoons olive oil

To make the chilli verde, place the pepper, chilli, coriander and spring onions in a liquidizer and blend to a coarse purée. Transfer to a mixing bowl, add the vinegar, mustard and oil. Season to taste. Leave at room temperature to allow the flavours to infuse.

Place the black beans in a saucepan, cover with cold water, add the garlic and cumin and bring to the boil. Reduce the heat and simmer gently for about 1 hour or until tender. Add the beer towards the end of the cooking time. When the beans are cooked, the liquid will have reduced and formed a sauce around them. Add the olive oil and season to taste.

Grill the chicken wings under a hot grill or over a barbecue. Arrange the wings on the black beans, drizzle over the chilli verde and serve hot.

Barbecue spice rub chicken

8 chicken thighs
8 chicken drumsticks

For the spice rub:
½ teaspoon salt
½ teaspoon sugar
½ teaspoon brown sugar
½ teaspoon dried chilli flakes
½ teaspoon black pepper
½ teaspoon paprika
¼ teaspoon ground cumin
¼ teaspoon cayenne pepper

Combine all the ingredients for the spice rub in a large bowl. Using a sharp knife, cut three incisions in each of the chicken pieces to allow the spices to permeate the flesh. Add the chicken to the dry ingredients and leave for 2 hours.

Cook on a barbecue or under a hot grill. Serve with a yoghurt and fresh herb dressing and a leafy mixed salad.

Turkey osso buco

1 large turkey leg, sawn through the bone into 5 cm (2 inch) 'steaks'
3–4 tablespoons flour
salt and freshly ground pepper
3 tablespoons vegetable oil
25 g (1 oz) butter
1 onion, finely chopped
2 carrots, cut into very small dice
2 sticks of celery, cut into very small dice
½ leek, cut into very small dice
1 garlic clove, crushed
1 tablespoon tomato purée
4 tablespoons dry white wine
2 tablespoons fresh orange juice
600 ml (1 pint) chicken stock

Preheat the oven to 160°C/325°F/Gas Mark 3.

Remove the sinews and any small bones from the turkey steaks. Coat the turkey with flour, seasoned with salt and pepper. Heat the oil in a saucepan or flameproof casserole wide enough to take the turkey steaks in one layer. Brown the turkey on both sides in the hot oil, then remove and set aside. Drain off any excess oil and add the butter to the pan.

Add the onion, carrots, celery, leek and garlic and cook over a low heat until the vegetables are tender. Add the tomato purée and stir in. Cook over a low heat for 2–3 minutes.

Add the wine and orange juice and boil for 3–4 minutes. Pour in the stock and return to the boil, adding a little salt and pepper.

Return the turkey to the pan, cover with a lid and place in the oven for 1–1½ hours. Alternatively, simmer on top of the cooker.

Serve hot, with seasonal vegetables and, if you like, risotto, which is the classic accompaniment to osso buco.

Spicy herb sausages in batter pudding

My version of an old British favourite, 'toad in the hole'.

450 g (1 lb) good-quality pork sausagemeat
1 tablespoon chopped fresh coriander
1 tablespoon fresh oregano leaves
¼ teaspoon dried chilli flakes
¼ teaspoon ground ginger
1 teaspoon mustard
4 spring onions, finely shredded
salt and freshly ground pepper
75 g (3 oz) plain flour
2 eggs
75 ml (3 fl oz) milk mixed with 50 ml (2 fl oz) water
3 tablespoons vegetable oil
2 tablespoons caraway seeds (optional)

Place the sausagemeat in a bowl and add the herbs, chilli, ginger, mustard and spring onions; mix in gently. Shape into eight small flat rounds and season with salt and pepper.

Sift the flour into a bowl, make a well in the centre, add the eggs and the milk and water and mix to form a paste. Beat until smooth, then strain and leave to stand for 30 minutes.

Preheat the oven to 200°C/400°F/Gas Mark 6. Grease one large baking tin or eight individual moulds with a little of the oil and place in the oven.

Heat the remaining oil in a frying pan and fry the sausage rounds for 1 minute on each side or until golden and sealed.

Pour the batter mix into the hot baking tin (or into the small moulds), add the sausage rounds and cook in the hot oven until risen and light in texture, about 30–35 minutes. If you like, sprinkle on the caraway seeds after about 20–25 minutes

Daube of rabbit with orange, cinnamon and rosemary

4 large fresh rabbit legs
salt and freshly ground pepper
½ tablespoon ground cinnamon
3–4 tablespoons flour
3 tablespoons olive oil
25 g (1 oz) butter
1 onion, finely chopped
1 garlic clove, crushed
1 tablespoon roughly chopped fresh rosemary
150 ml (5 fl oz) red wine
600 ml (1 pint) chicken stock
200 g (7 oz) canned tomatoes, chopped
50 ml (2 fl oz) orange juice
sugar

Preheat the oven to 180°C/350°F/Gas Mark 4.

Season the rabbit legs with salt, pepper and cinnamon. Dust them in the flour. Heat the oil in a flameproof casserole, add the rabbit legs and fry until golden and sealed. Remove from the pan and set aside.

Drain off any excess fat, add the butter and the onion and cook over a low heat until tender. Add the garlic and rosemary and cook for a further 1 minute. Pour in the red wine and bring to the boil, then add the stock and reduce the heat.

Return the legs to the sauce, add the chopped tomatoes, orange juice, a good pinch of sugar and a little salt and pepper. Cover with a lid and cook in the oven for 1 hour or until tender. Serve with polenta beaten with plenty of butter.

Braised blade of pork

If you can arrange your oven to take two casserole dishes, this satisfying dinner is even easier and more economical.

600 g (1¼ lb) blade of pork, boneless
6 dried prunes, soaked overnight and drained
salt and freshly ground pepper
2 tablespoons vegetable oil
300 ml (½ pint) red wine
1 litre (1¾ pints) chicken stock

For the red cabbage:
1 red cabbage, about 400 g (14 oz)
100 g (4 oz) butter
4 tablespoons white wine vinegar
15 g (½ oz) sugar
3 tablespoons redcurrant jelly

Preheat the oven to 200°C/400°F/Gas Mark 6. Take a knife or, better still, a kitchen steel and push a hole through the centre of the pork. Fill the hole with the soaked prunes, pushing them in with your fingers. Season the pork with salt and pepper.

Heat the oil in flameproof casserole and fry the pork until golden and sealed on all sides.

Drain off the excess oil, then pour in the wine and bring to the boil for 2 minutes. Pour in the stock, cover with a tight-fitting lid and place in the hot oven for 1½ hours or until tender. During the cooking, baste the pork several times with the wine and stock.

Cut the cabbage into quarters, remove the central core and the faded outside leaves. Cut the cabbage into fine shreds. Heat the butter in a saucepan or flameproof casserole, add the cabbage, vinegar, sugar and 600 ml (1 pint) water. Bring to the boil, then cover with a lid and simmer for 45 minutes–1 hour. Alternatively, cook in the oven with the pork.When the cabbage is tender, remove the lid and boil to reduce any remaining liquid to a syrup. Add the redcurrant jelly to form a light glaze around the cabbage and season to taste.

To serve, slice the braised pork and serve on the cabbage, with some of the braising juices poured over. A tart apple purée goes well with this dish.

Chocolate chilli glazed pork

675 g (1½ lb) pork belly, cut into strips
salt and freshly ground pepper
4 fresh red chillies, deseeded
2 tablespoons clear honey, warmed
50 g (2 oz) bitter chocolate, melted

Preheat the oven to 200°C/400°F/Gas Mark 6. Season the pork, then roast in the hot oven for 30–35 minutes or until golden.

Meanwhile, in a liquidizer, blend the chillies and the honey; pour into a bowl, add the melted chocolate and mix well.

Remove the pork from the oven, drain on paper towels, brush with the chocolate glaze and return to the oven for 10 minutes.

Serve on a bed of crisp mixed vegetables stir-fried with a little chopped fresh ginger.

Korean-style barbecue lamb ribs

16 lamb ribs
salt and freshly ground pepper
4 tablespoons tomato ketchup
6 tablespoons soy sauce
½ tablespoon mustard
1 garlic clove, crushed
1 tablespoon sugar
1 tablespoon white wine vinegar
½ teaspoon ground ginger
3 teaspoons sesame seeds

Season the ribs with salt and pepper. Combine all the remaining ingredients together and coat the ribs in the mixture. Leave to marinate for up to 2 hours.

Place on a barbecue and grill for 20–25 minutes or until tender and slightly burnt on the edges. Alternatively, cook in a hot oven at 200°C/400°F/Gas Mark 6.

Persian koftas with pitta toasts

400 g (14 oz) lean minced lamb
50 g (2 oz) cooked rice
1 onion, finely chopped or grated
1 teaspoon ground cinnamon
1 teaspoon ground cumin
salt and freshly ground pepper
2 eggs, beaten
3–4 tablespoons seasoned flour
75 g (3 oz) butter
1 tablespoon olive oil
4 pitta breads

For the salad:
75 g (3 oz) cucumber, cut into 1 cm (½ inch) dice
1 red onion, cut into 1 cm (½ inch) dice
½ garlic clove, crushed
4 tomatoes, deseeded, and cut into 1 cm (½ inch) dice
4 tablespoons olive oil
juice of ½ lemon
2 tablespoons fresh coriander, chopped

Place the minced lamb in a bowl, add the rice, onion, spices, salt and pepper and mix well. Add one of the eggs to bind the mixture. Wetting your hands with water, shape the lamb mixture into oval balls. Place in the refrigerator until ready to cook.

For the salad, mix all the ingredients together; season to taste.

When ready to cook, soak eight or more bamboo skewers in cold water for 30 minutes. Preheat the grill or barbecue. Roll the meatballs in the seasoned flour, then in the remaining beaten egg. Thread them on to the skewers and grill, turning from time to time, until cooked and browned, about 15 minutes. Alternatively, heat the oil and butter in a frying pan and fry the meatballs until crisp and browned. Toast the pitta breads and fill with the koftas and salad.

VEGETARIAN DISHES

Potato tortilla with rosemary and lemon

275 g (10 oz) new potatoes
salt and freshly ground pepper
1 garlic clove, halved
6 tablespoons olive oil
1 tablespoon chopped fresh rosemary
grated zest of ½ lemon
5 eggs
2 spring onions, shredded

Place the potatoes in a saucepan, cover with cold water, add salt and bring to the boil. Reduce the heat and cook until just tender. Drain and leave to cool.

When cold, cut the potatoes into thick slices. Rub a 20 cm (8 inch) omelette pan with the garlic clove. Heat 4 tablespoons of the oil, add the potato slices and cook over a low heat until golden. Add half the rosemary and the lemon zest and toss well to mix.

Beat the eggs in a bowl, season with salt and pepper and add the spring onions. Pour the mixture over the potatoes and cook over a fairly high heat for 1 minute or until the egg sets underneath. Carefully turn the omelette over and cook the other side. Sprinkle over the remaining rosemary and drizzle on the remaining oil; serve warm.

Leeks Portuguese

6 tablespoons olive oil
1 onion, finely sliced
1 garlic clove, crushed
450 g (1 lb) young leeks, about 10 cm (4 inches) long, trimmed
3 tablespoons white wine
150 ml (¼ pint) vegetable stock
6 coriander seeds, crushed
200 g (7 oz) canned tomatoes, roughly chopped
sugar
salt and coarsely ground black pepper

Heat the olive oil in a wide saucepan, add the onion and garlic and cook over a low heat until tender. Add the leeks and cook for 2 minutes, then pour in the white wine. Bring to the boil and boil for 1 minute, then add the stock. Cover with a lid and simmer gently for 5–10 minutes or until the leeks are tender but not broken up. Using a slotted spoon, remove the leeks and set aside.

Add the coriander seeds and tomatoes to the cooking liquid and boil for 5–10 minutes or until thickened and slightly reduced. Season to taste with a pinch of sugar, salt and pepper. Return the leeks to the liquid and leave to cool.

Serve at room temperature, sprinkled with coarsely ground black pepper.

Muffin pizzas

A simple, convenient and delicious alternative to the pizza base, with some of my favourite toppings listed below.

8 muffins
olive oil

Halve the muffins, brush with olive oil and toast them lightly under a hot grill, then add your choice of topping.

Garlic mushroom

200 g (7 oz) canned tomatoes, drained and chopped
2 tablespoons olive oil
1 garlic clove, crushed
100 g (4 oz) button mushrooms, sliced
1 tablespoon capers
fresh or dried oregano
salt and freshly ground pepper

Place the tomatoes in a small saucepan and cook over a high heat until they become quite thick and pulpy. Leave to cool.

Heat the oil in a frying pan, add the garlic and mushrooms and cook for 2 minutes. Add the capers and oregano, mix together and season to taste. Spread the toasted muffins with the tomato mixture, then top with the mushrooms. Place under a hot grill for 3–4 minutes.

Napoletana

8 fresh ripe tomatoes
2 tablespoons olive oil
1 onion, chopped
4–5 fresh sage leaves, chopped
50 g (2 oz) black olives, pitted and chopped
2 anchovy fillets, drained and chopped (optional for vegetarians!)
Cheddar cheese, grated

Cut the tomatoes into 5 mm ($^1/_4$ inch) slices. Heat the oil in a small frying pan and add the onion, sage, olives and anchovies, if using. Cook until the onion is tender.

Arrange the tomato slices on the toasted muffins, spoon on the olive mixture, then top with grated cheese. Place under a hot grill for 3–4 minutes or until golden and bubbling.

Blue cheese and walnut

4 tablespoons olive oil
1 red onion, thinly sliced
$^1/_4$ teaspoon dried sage
100 g (4 oz) blue cheese (e.g. Gorgonzola)
2 tablespoons milk
2 tablespoons walnuts, toasted and roughly chopped

Heat 3 tablespoons of the oil in a saucepan over a low heat, add the onion and sage and cook until tender but not browned. Leave to cool.

Mash the cheese with the milk to make a smooth spread. Mix in the walnuts and the cooled onions. Chill.

Spread the mixture over the toasted muffins and place under a hot grill until golden.

Chilli bean

1 tablespoon vegetable oil
$^1/_2$ onion, chopped
$^1/_4$ teaspoon dried chilli flakes
1 teaspoon ground cumin
1 tablespoon chopped fresh coriander
400 g (14 oz) canned black beans, chopped
$^1/_2$ avocado, sliced
2 tablespoons sour cream
2 tablespoons grated Cheddar cheese

Heat the oil in a small frying pan over a low heat, add the onion, chilli, cumin and coriander and cook until the onion is tender. Add the chopped black beans and continue cooking over low heat until the mixture is quite thick.

Spread the beans on the toasted muffins and top with the avocado, sour cream and grated cheese.

Lentil moussaka tart

175 g (6 oz) lentils, soaked overnight
8 tablespoons vegetable oil
1 onion, finely chopped
1 garlic clove, crushed
1 teaspoon dried thyme
1 teaspoon ground allspice
2 tablespoons tomato purée
2 tablespoons flour
salt and freshly ground pepper
1 large aubergine
1 potato, thinly sliced
1 x 22 cm (9 inch) cooked shortcrust pastry shell

For the cheese sauce:
25 g (1 oz) butter
25 g (1 oz) flour
250 ml (8 fl oz) milk
1 teaspoon mustard
50 g (2 oz) cheese, grated

Cook the lentils in about 600 ml (1 pint) water for 30–40 minutes or until tender. Drain and reserve the cooking liquid; you should have about 300 ml (½ pint).

Heat 2 tablespoons of the oil in a saucepan, add the onion and garlic and cook gently until tender. Increase the heat, add the cooked lentils, the thyme, allspice and tomato purée and mix well. Cook for a further 2 minutes. Add the flour and mix in well. Pour in the reserved lentil cooking liquid a little at a time to form a sauce around the lentils. Simmer for 10–15 minutes or until the sauce becomes quite thick. Season to taste and leave to cool.

Preheat the oven to 200°C/400°F/Gas Mark 6. Make the cheese sauce, following the method on page 89, and beating in the mustard and cheese at the end.

Slice the aubergine lengthways into 1 cm (½ inch) thick slices. Fry in the remaining oil until golden and tender. Drain on paper towels and season lightly. Parboil the potato slices for 2–3 minutes, drain and pat dry. Fill each aubergine slice with the lentil mixture, roll them up and place them in the pastry shell. Arrange the potato slices in overlapping rows over the aubergine to cover the tart. Pour the sauce over the potatoes, then place the tart into a hot oven for 15–20 minutes or until bubbling and golden.

Winter vegetable goulash

4 tablespoons olive oil
1 small cauliflower, cut into florets
3 carrots, cut into 5 mm (¼ inch) slices
2 tablespoons butter
1 tablespoon caraway seeds
1 garlic clove, crushed
2 turnips, cut into 5 mm (¼ inch) slices
1 swede, cut into 5 mm (¼ inch) slices
1 teaspoon paprika
1 tablespoon tomato purée
1 tablespoon flour
150 ml (¼ pint) dry white wine
600 ml (1 pint) vegetable stock
2 courgettes, cut into 5 mm (¼ inch) slices
1 leek, cut into 5 mm (¼ inch) slices
salt and freshly ground pepper

Heat 3 tablespoons of the oil in a heavy-bottomed saucepan, add the cauliflower and carrots and cook gently for 2 minutes, without letting them brown.

Add the butter, caraway seeds and garlic and cook for 1 minute, then add the turnip and swede. Sprinkle over the paprika to coat the vegetables. Stir in the tomato purée and flour and cook over a low heat for 2–3 minutes.

Pour in the wine, bring to the boil, and add the vegetable stock. Simmer until the vegetables are just cooked, but still slightly crisp.

Add the courgettes and leek and cook for 2 minutes. Finally add the remaining olive oil. Serve at once, with noodles or rice.

Lentil koftas

150 g (5 oz) lentils, soaked overnight
4 tablespoons vegetable oil
1 green chilli, deseeded and chopped
1 garlic clove, crushed
3 spring onions, shredded
1 tablespoon ground cumin
½ tablespoon ground coriander
salt and freshly ground pepper
4 tablespoons rye flour (or plain flour)

For the raita:
1 stick of celery, cut into small dice
75 g (3 oz) cucumber, peeled and cut into small dice
2 tomatoes, halved and cut into small dice
100 ml (3 fl oz) natural yoghurt
2 tablespoons chopped fresh mint

Start making this dish the day before you want to serve it. Place the lentils in a saucepan, cover with cold water and bring to the boil. Skim off any impurities from the surface of the water, then reduce the heat and cook for 30–40 minutes or until tender. Drain well.

Heat half the oil in a frying pan, add the lentils, chilli and garlic and fry until dry. Add the spring onions, cumin, coriander, salt and pepper and cook for a further 2 minutes.

Add the flour, mix well and cook over a low heat for 3–4 minutes. Leave to cool, then place in the refrigerator overnight.

To make the raita, mix all the ingredients together and chill. Alternatively, make the fruit raita on page 44.

To cook the koftas, heat the remaining oil in a frying pan. Shape the lentil mixture into small ovals and fry gently until golden, about 2 minutes on each side. Serve hot, with the chilled raita.

Savoy cabbage and parsnip jalousie

1 Savoy cabbage
50 g (2 oz) butter
1 onion, thinly sliced
1 teaspoon sugar
1 teaspoon mustard
salt and freshly ground pepper
450 g (1 lb) parsnips, coarsely grated
2 tablespoons caraway seeds
100 g (4 oz) cooked brown rice
50 g (2 oz) Cheddar cheese, grated
2 eggs, beaten
325 g (12 oz) puff pastry
flour for rolling

Remove the outer leaves from the cabbage, blanch them in boiling salted water for 3–4 minutes, refresh under cold water and then dry them well. Roughly shred the remainder of the cabbage.

Heat half the butter in a small frying pan, add the onion and sugar and cook until golden and caramelized. Remove from the heat and leave to cool, then add the mustard and season to taste.

Heat the remaining butter in a frying pan, add the shredded cabbage, grated parsnip and 1 tablespoon caraway seeds, fry for 3–4 minutes or until softened. Transfer to a bowl and leave to cool. Add the rice and cheese and bind the mixture together with one of the eggs.

Preheat the oven to 190°C/375°F/Gas Mark 5.

On a lightly floured surface, roll out the pastry to measure about 20 x 30 cm (8 by 12 inches). Arrange the outer cabbage leaves on the pastry, leaving a 2.5 cm (1 inch) border around the edge. Top with the shredded cabbage mixture. Spoon the caramelized onions along the centre of the filling.

Fold the pastry over and press the edges to seal well. Very carefully lift the pastry roll on to a baking sheet, turning the seam underneath. Brush the pastry all over with the remaining beaten egg and decorate with any pastry trimmings. Brush again with egg, then sprinkle with the remaining caraway seeds. Bake for 20–25 minutes or until cooked and golden brown.

PUDDINGS

Sweet raisin fougasse

15 g (½ oz) fresh yeast
450 g (1 lb) flour, sifted
50 g (2 oz) sugar
2 tablespoons olive oil
225 g (8 oz) raisins, soaked in water
1 tablespoon clear honey

Dissolve the yeast in 300 ml (½ pint) warm water and leave for 5 minutes. Mix the flour with the sugar in a large bowl.

Add the oil to the yeast mixture, then add to the flour and mix to form a smooth dough. Leave to rise in a warm, draught-free place for up to 1 hour or until doubled in size.

Pat the raisins dry on paper towels and work into the dough, then leave for a further 30 minutes.

Preheat the oven to 200°C/400°F/Gas Mark 6. Lightly grease a baking sheet. Form the dough into a flat oval shape, place on the baking sheet and bake for about 30 minutes, until risen and golden. Brush with the honey as soon as it comes out of the oven. Leave to cool before serving with lashings of fresh cream. Alternatively this can be made in a loaf tin – and it makes great toast!

Baked plums in red wine syrup

12 ripe Victoria plums, halved and stoned
75 g (3 oz) sugar
150 ml (¼ pint) red wine
juice and grated zest of 1 orange
½ bay leaf
2 cloves

Preheat the oven to 150°C/300°F/Gas Mark 2.

Place the plums in an ovenproof dish and sprinkle with the sugar. Place the wine in a saucepan with the orange juice and zest, bay leaf, cloves and 2 tablespoons water, bring to the boil, boil for 2 minutes, then pour over the plums. Bake for 15–20 minutes or until the plums are tender and the cooking liquid has formed a syrup. (It may be necessary to remove the plums and transfer the liquid to a saucepan to boil until reduced to a coating consistency.)

Serve warm or cold – excellent with vanilla ice cream.

Cinnamon baked apples 'en papillote'

These apples formed part of the original £1 menu for four that sparked off the idea for this book.

75 g (3 oz) butter
75 g (3 oz) sugar
½ teaspoon ground cinnamon
2 drops of vanilla essence
juice of ½ orange
4 ripe yellow Golden Delicious apples

Preheat the oven to 190°C/375° F/Gas Mark 5.

Melt the butter in a saucepan, add the sugar, cinnamon, vanilla essence, orange juice and 4 tablespoons water and boil until caramelized to a light sticky syrup.

Core the apples with an apple corer or a melon baller and make a few incisions in the skins to prevent the apples from bursting while they are cooking.

Butter a sheet of foil about 38 cm (15 inches) square and place on a baking sheet (the edges will be overhanging at this stage). Lay the apples on the foil, leaving a gap of about 4 cm (1½ inches) between them. Brush the syrup over the apples, bring the foil up to the top and seal together. Place in the oven and bake for 20–25 minutes or until the apples are tender.

Bring the foil parcel to the table and then undo the foil to release the aroma. Serve the apples with the cooking juices poured over them.

Double orange pudding

150 ml (¼ pint) milk
100 g (4 oz) sugar
½ teaspoon vanilla essence
juice and grated zest of 1 orange
40 g (1½ oz) butter
40 g (1½ oz) flour
3 eggs, separated
6 tablespoons coarse orange marmalade

Preheat the oven to 180°C/350°F/Gas Mark 4. Lightly butter four individual ramekin or pudding moulds (or teacups), about 150 ml (¼ pint) each.

Bring the milk to the boil with half the sugar, the vanilla essence and orange zest, then leave to cool slightly.

In another saucepan, melt the butter and stir in the flour to form a smooth paste. Cook over a low heat for about 1 minute, stirring constantly, then gradually pour in the warm milk, beating well until smooth. Add the orange juice and cook the sauce over a low heat for 5–8 minutes, then leave to cool slightly before beating in the egg yolks.

Whisk the whites until stiff, then fold in the remaining sugar. Beat half the whites into the sauce, then carefully fold the sauce into the remaining whites until evenly combined. Divide the mixture between the buttered moulds, but do not overfill them: they should be about two-thirds full.

Place the moulds in a roasting tin with about 2 cm (¾ inch) hot water in the bottom and cook for 20 minutes or until risen and set.

Meanwhile, heat the marmalade in a small saucepan with 6 tablespoons water to form a sauce.

Turn the puddings out on to warmed serving plates and serve at once, with the sauce poured over them. For an elegant presentation, decorate with orange segments and sprigs of mint.

Apple bread and butter pudding

4 tablespoons melted butter
4 slices of white bread (or 4 white crusty rolls)
2 yellow Golden Delicious apples, cored and thinly sliced
100 g (4 oz) raisins
600 ml (1 pint) milk
½ teaspoon vanilla essence
4 eggs
4 tablespoons sugar
2 tablespoons apricot jam, warmed
icing sugar to dust

Preheat the oven to 160°C/325°F/Gas Mark 3. Butter an ovenproof pudding dish.

Butter the bread, then cut each slice into four triangles; if using rolls, cut them into 5 mm ($^1/_4$ inch) thick slices. Arrange the bread in the pudding dish, overlapping neatly, with the thinly sliced apple between the slices of bread. Sprinkle over the raisins and set aside.

Bring the milk to the boil with the vanilla essence.

In a bowl, beat the eggs with the sugar, then carefully pour on the hot milk, a little at a time, whisking continuously until the mixture forms a smooth custard. Strain the custard, then pour it over the bread.

Place the pudding dish in a roasting tin containing about 2.5 cm (1 inch) boiling water and bake for 40 minutes or until just firm to the touch. Remove from the oven and leave to cool slightly. Brush with the apricot jam. Just before serving, dust with a little icing sugar.

Prune and almond frittata

100 g (4 oz) dried prunes, stones removed, soaked overnight in cold tea
50 g (2 oz) butter
4 tablespoons brandy (optional luxury)
6 eggs, beaten
4 tablespoons sugar
4 tablespoons ground almonds
2 tablespoons flaked almonds
Icing sugar to glaze

Preheat the grill.

Cut the prunes into quarters and pat them dry. Heat the butter in an omelette pan about 15 cm (6 inches) in diameter. Add the prunes and heat through for 1 minute. Add the brandy, if using, and ignite. Shake the pan until the flames die down.

In a bowl, beat the eggs with the sugar and ground almonds. Pour the egg mixture on to the prunes and stir gently with a fork over a fairly high heat until lightly set. Sprinkle over the flaked almonds and dust with plenty of icing sugar. Place the pan under the hot grill until the icing sugar forms a golden glaze.

Turn out onto a warmed serving plate, dust with a little more icing sugar and serve at once, with a big spoonful of crème fraîche.

Cinnamon and lemon fritters

6 tablespoons milk
juice and grated zest of 1 lemon
3 tablespoons butter
¼ teaspoon salt
250 g (9 oz) sugar
90 g (3½ oz) plain flour, sifted
2 eggs
vegetable oil for deep-frying
1 teaspoon ground cinnamon

Place the milk, lemon zest, butter, salt and half the sugar in a saucepan and bring to the boil. Add the flour all at once and beat to a smooth paste, using a wooden spoon. Reduce the heat and continue beating until the dough leaves the sides of the pan clean. Leave to cool slightly, then add the eggs one at a time, beating well after each addition.

Heat the oil for deep-frying to 180°C/350°F (until a cube of bread browns in 30 seconds).

Carefully drop teaspoonfuls of the mixture into the hot oil and cook for 4–5 minutes until golden. It is best not to cook too many spoonfuls in each batch. Drain the fritters on paper towels. Mix the remaining sugar with the cinnamon and roll the hot fritters in the cinnamon sugar. Serve hot with vanilla ice cream.

Caramelized bananas with coconut fried ice cream

500 ml (16 fl oz) vanilla ice cream
1 egg, beaten
75 g (3 oz) flour, sifted
4 tablespoons desiccated coconut
4 tablespoons fresh white breadcrumbs
4 bananas
6 tablespoons maple syrup
6 tablespoons orange juice
2 tablespoons fresh lemon juice
2 tablespoons rum (optional luxury)
vegetable oil for deep-frying

Prepare the ice cream the day before you want to serve this dish. Using an ice cream scoop, scoop four balls of ice cream. and place in the freezer on a sheet of foil. Prepare a thick batter by beating together the egg, flour and 4–5 tablespoons water. Mix the desiccated coconut with the breadcrumbs in a shallow dish. Dip the ice cream balls in the batter, then roll them in the coconut mixture to coat them thickly and evenly, Return to the freezer and freeze overnight.

When required, peel the bananas and cut each one in half lengthways. Heat the maple syrup, orange and lemon juice, and rum, if using, in a frying pan over a moderate heat. Add the bananas and cook for 3–4 minutes, adding a little water if necessary, so that the bananas are caramelized, warmed through and surrounded by a light syrup.

Heat the oil until a cube of bread browns in 30 seconds. Fry the ice cream balls until they are just golden. Serve at once, with the bananas and the caramelized juices.

Banana 'Wednesday'

Why save a sundae for Sunday?

4 bananas
40 g (1½ oz) soft brown sugar
3 tablespoons double cream
40 g (1½ oz) unsalted butter
¼ teaspoon vanilla essence
4 scoops of chocolate ice cream
1 tablespoon flaked almonds
sprigs of mint to decorate

Preheat the oven to 200°C/400°F/Gas Mark 6.

Place the bananas on a baking sheet and bake for 5–8 minutes or until they are warmed through but not soft.

Meanwhile, prepare the sauce. Place the sugar, cream, butter and vanilla essence in a heavy-bottomed saucepan and cook, stirring for 3–5 minutes or until the mixture turns a light caramel colour.

Peel the bananas and cut them in half lengthways or into slices.

Place the chocolate ice cream in individual dishes, top with the roasted bananas and pour over the caramel sauce. Sprinkle over the toasted almonds and decorate with the mint.

Sweetcorn ice cream with summer berry compote

3 egg yolks
1 egg
150 g (5 oz) sugar
400 ml (14 fl oz) milk
200 ml (7 fl oz) double cream
175 g (6 oz) canned sweetcorn kernels, puréed

For the compote:
3 tablespoons sugar
400 g (14 oz) mixed berries (strawberries, blackberries, raspberries)
sprigs of mint to decorate

To make the ice cream, whisk the egg yolks, egg and sugar until pale in colour and doubled in volume. Boil the milk and cream together, then leave to cool slightly. Pour the milk a little at a time on to the egg mixture, stirring all the time. Add the puréed sweetcorn and strain through a sieve.

Return the mixture to the saucepan and cook over a low heat, stirring constantly, until the mixture thickens enough to coat the back of a spoon (do not let it boil.)

Cool the mixture quickly. When cold, pour into an ice cream machine and freeze. When the ice cream is set, transfer it to a plastic container and place in the freezer.

To make the compote, place the sugar in a saucepan with 3 tablespoons water, bring to the boil, add the berries and remove from the heat. Cover and leave to cool completely.

Before serving let the ice cream soften a little at room temperature. Spoon the fruit compote into individual soup plates. Top with a ball of the sweetcorn ice cream and decorate with sprigs of mint.

Asian toffee rice pudding

50 g (2 oz) butter
75 g (3 oz) demerara sugar
¼ teaspoon ground cinnamon
10 cardamom pods, shelled and seeds crushed
pinch of freshly grated nutmeg
75 g (3 oz) ground rice
1 litre (1¾ pints) milk
25 g (1 oz) sultanas

Heat the butter and sugar together in a saucepan until slightly caramelized. Add the spices and the rice and stir well.

Add the milk a little at a time, stirring well to prevent lumps from forming. When all the milk has been added, reduce the heat, add the sultanas and cook over a low heat for about 25 minutes. If the pudding becomes too thick, add a little more milk. Serve hot or cold. I particularly like this dessert served cold with a compote of apricots, topped with toasted almonds.

Poached pears in espresso-cardamom syrup

4 firm but ripe dessert pears (preferably Williams)
300 ml (½ pint) strong coffee (espresso)
150 g (5 oz) sugar
6 cardamom pods, crushed
juice and grated zest of ½ lemon
2 tablespoons flaked almonds, toasted
sprigs of mint to decorate

Peel the pears neatly, using a potato peeler, leaving the stalks intact and keeping the shape of the pear. Cut a little off the base of each pear to help it remain upright while it is poaching.

Choose a saucepan that will hold the four pears upright side by side. Put the coffee, sugar, 75 ml (3 fl oz) water, cardamom and the the lemon juice and zest in the pan and bring to the boil, stirring until the sugar has dissolved. Add the pears, cover the pan, reduce the heat and simmer for about 20–25 minutes or until the pears are tender but still retaining their shape.

Using a slotted spoon, remove the pears from the syrup and transfer to a bowl. Boil the syrup rapidly until reduced to about 125 ml (4 fl oz). Leave to cool, then pour the syrup over the pears and place in the refrigerator for up to 4 hours, to chill thoroughly.

Serve the pears with the coffee syrup, sprinkle over the toasted almonds and decorate with the mint. Serve with crème fraîche or vanilla yoghurt.

Lemonade granita with raspberry sauce

6 juicy lemons
150 g (5 oz) sugar
225 g (8 oz) can raspberries (or fresh, in season)
1 tablespoon caster sugar
raspberries and sprigs of mint to decorate

Finely grate the zest of one of the lemons. Squeeze the juice from all the lemons. Place the sugar, 450 ml ($^3/_4$ pint) water and the lemon zest in a saucepan, bring to the boil, reduce the heat and simmer until the sugar has dissolved. Add the lemon juice and leave to cool.

Pour the liquid into a shallow dish (preferably stainless steel) approximately 15 cm (6 inches) square and place in the freezer.

After 30 minutes or so the liquid will start to set on the surface and around the edge of the dish. Using a fork, scrape it until the loose crystals of ice are evenly distributed. Return to the freezer for a further 30 minutes. Repeat the scraping process twice more.

Place the raspberries in a liquidizer with the caster sugar and blend to a purée. Rub through a sieve to remove any pips.

To serve, scoop the lemon granita into individual glasses, pour over the raspberry sauce and decorate with raspberries and mint.

Blackberry ice cream soda

I'm sure many of you remember enjoying ice cream soda when you were young. Here is a real taste of nostalgia and late-summer simplicity.

325 g (12 oz) fresh blackberries (buy or pick your own)
a little caster sugar
4 scoops of vanilla ice cream
300 ml (½ pint) cream soda

Sweeten the blackberries with a little sugar if required. Divide the berries between four tall glasses and top with the ice cream. Pour over the soda and serve immediately, while it is still bubbling.

INDEX

Acknowledgements

A million thanks to my wife, Anita, whose help and patience behind the scenes has been truly invaluable, and to my children Lee, Ryan, Lauren and Rosie, to whom the book is dedicated.

I would very much like to thank the following people for their invaluable contributions to this book:

Bridget Sargeson and Jane Suthering, food stylists, and Julian Marshall, my executive sous-chef, who between them prepared the dishes for photography; I thank them all immensely.

Photographer Philip Wilkins, for the care and true professionalism that went into each photograph, which is evident in the final product.

Sue Russell, for her beautiful photographic props and materials.

All at Weidenfeld & Nicolson, particularly Nick Clark and Maggie Ramsay, and Editorial Director Susan Haynes, for her belief and interest in the idea.

Geoffrey Gelardi, Managing Director at The Lanesborough, for his continuing support and encouragement in my new projects.

Finally, I must not forget to thank Simon Hinde, Consumer Affairs Correspondent for the *Sunday Times*, who set the challenge in 1995 that set the whole idea of this book in motion.